WORLD EXPLORERS

Discover the Past

by Denise Bieniek, M.S.
Illustrated by Patrick Girouard
This edition published in 2002.

10 9 8 7 6 5

Troll!
CREATIVE
▲▲▲▲▲▲▲▲▲▲▲▲▲▲▲▲▲▲▲
TEACHER

IDEAS

D1401458

Troll Creative Teacher Ideas was designed to help today's dedicated, time-pressured teacher. Created by teachers for teachers, this innovative series provides a wealth of classroom ideas to help reinforce important concepts and stimulate your students' creative thinking skills.

Each book in the series focuses on a different curriculum theme to give you the flexibility to teach any given skill at any time of the year. The wide range of ideas and activities included in each book are certain to help you create an atmosphere where students are continually eager to learn new concepts and develop important skills.

We hope this comprehensive series will provide you with everything you need to foster a fun and challenging learning environment for your students. **Troll Creative Teacher Ideas** is a resource you'll turn to again and again!

Titles in this series:

Classroom Decor:
Decorate Your Classroom from Bulletin Boards to Time Lines

Creative Projects: Quick and Easy Art Projects

Earth Alert: Environmental Studies for Grades 4-6

Explore the World: Social Studies Projects and Activities

Healthy Bodies, Healthy Minds

Holidays Around the World: Multicultural Projects and Activities

It All Adds Up: Math Skill-Building Activities for Grades 4-6

Learning Through Literature:
Projects and Activities for Linking Literature and Writing

Story Writing: Creative Writing Projects and Activities

Think About It: Skill-Building Puzzles Across the Curriculum

The World Around Us: Geography Projects and Activities

World Explorers: Discover the Past

Metric Conversion Chart

1 inch = 2.54 cm	1 foot = .305 m	1 yard = .914 m
1 mile = 1.61 km	1 fluid ounce = 29.573 ml	1 cup = .24 l
1 pint = .473 l	1 teaspoon = 4.93 ml	1 tablespoon = 14.78 ml

Contents

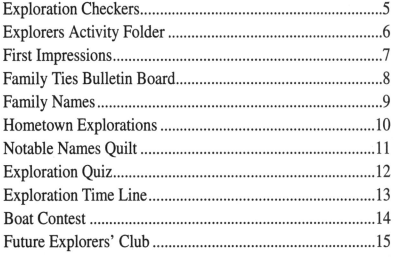

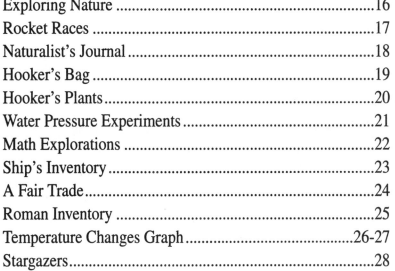
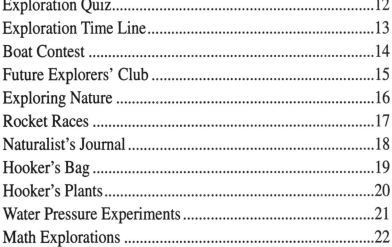
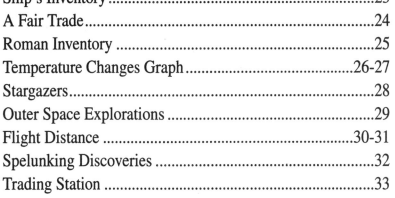

Exploration Checkers

MATERIALS:

3" x 5" index cards
scissors
crayons or markers
tape
checkerboard and checkers

DIRECTIONS:

1. Have two volunteers lay out a checkerboard and checkers as if to begin a traditional game of checkers.
2. Cut index cards into 20 squares small enough to fit on top of the squares on a checkerboard.
3. On each square, write an explorer's name. The explorers named may be men or women, famous or little-known, or from any area of exploration. On the back of each square, indicate what the explorer was known for.
4. Lay the index card squares faceup randomly onto any of the squares of a checkerboard that are not covered by game pieces at the start of the game.
5. Instruct the two volunteers to begin playing a traditional game of checkers. But whenever a player's piece is to be moved onto a square covered by a name, he or she must identify the explorer by telling what the explorer is known for.
6. If a player cannot identify an explorer's name, he or she may not make the intended move or jump. The winner is the player with the most pieces after the last index card square has been turned over.

Explorers Activity Folder

MATERIALS:

8" x 10" pieces of oaktag
crayons or markers
old magazines
scissors
glue
pocket folder

DIRECTIONS:

1. On each of several 8" x 10" pieces of oaktag, draw a picture of a form of transportation that has been used to explore the world (e.g., a ship). Or cut out pictures from magazines that show such a form of transportation and glue one on the oaktag sheet.

2. At the top of each piece of oaktag, write two clues about an explorer who used the transportation featured. Make clues difficult or easy, depending on the knowledge of the students.

3. At the bottom of the oaktag sheets, write two letters from the featured explorers' names, leaving a short blank line for each missing letter.

4. On the back of the pieces of oaktag, write the featured explorers' names.

5. Demonstrate to the class how to use the activity. Ask each student to read the clues at the top of a sheet, look at the form of transportation that is most associated with the chosen explorer and at the letters of the name provided, and then figure out his or her name based on this information. To check answers, students may look at the back of the sheets.

6. Place all the pieces of oaktag in the pockets of a folder. Place the folder in the social studies center for student use during free time.

7. Students may wish to make explorer riddles of their own. Encourage the children to think of new explorers and place their riddles in the activity folder with the others.

First Impressions

Name _____

Think of a place you would be interested in exploring. Then research your choice to discover what it was like when it was first explored and what it is like today. What things are different? What things are the same?

Fill in the Venn diagram below with your research information. Share your findings with the class.

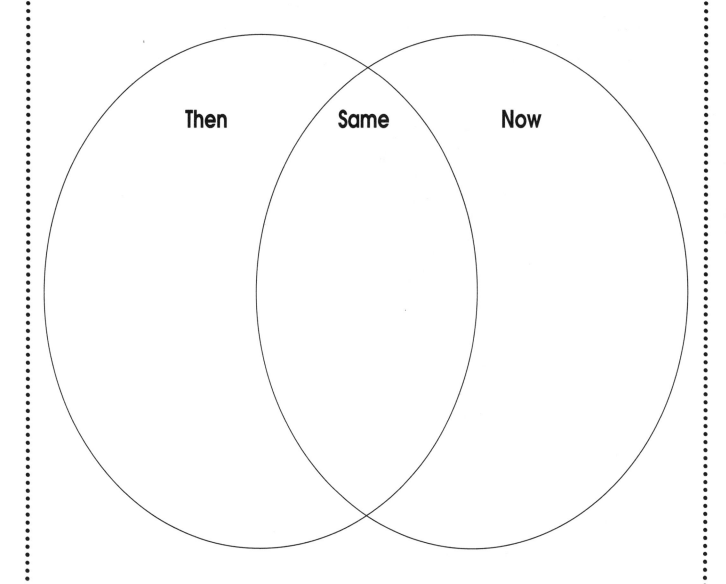

Then   **Same**   **Now**

Family Ties Bulletin Board

MATERIALS:

bulletin board paper
stapler
construction paper
glue

DIRECTIONS:

1. Ask students to brainstorm on the topic of immigration. They may give reasons why people might immigrate, discuss periods of increased immigration, or name problems people might encounter when they move from one country to another.

2. Have students identify categories among the answers and then try to group the answers under the category headings.

3. Encourage students to explain some of their comments. Ask if any of their relatives were, or are, immigrants and whether these relatives might like to share their experiences with the class.

4. Ask the children to guess when their relatives came to settle in the country in which they now live. See if any students still have relatives living in the family's country of origin. Help students make up a questionnaire designed to find the answers to the above questions, as well as other interesting facts about their families.

5. Compare and contrast answers to the questionnaires when they are completed. If possible, invite relatives into the classroom to talk about their experiences of immigration with the class.

6. Demonstrate to the class how to construct a family tree. In each space, have them include the name of a relative, his or her relationship to them, where he or she was born, and where he or she lives now.

7. Cover a bulletin board with bright paper. Mount the students' work on colorful construction paper and display the family trees on the bulletin board with the title "Family Ties."

Family Names

Name

_____

In Iceland today, as elsewhere in Scandinavia long ago, there is an interesting way of naming children. A female child's last name is her father's first name in the possessive with the word _dottir_ ("daughter") attached to it. A male child's last name is his father's first name in the possessive with the word _son_ ("son") attached to it.

Here is an example of an Icelandic family tree:

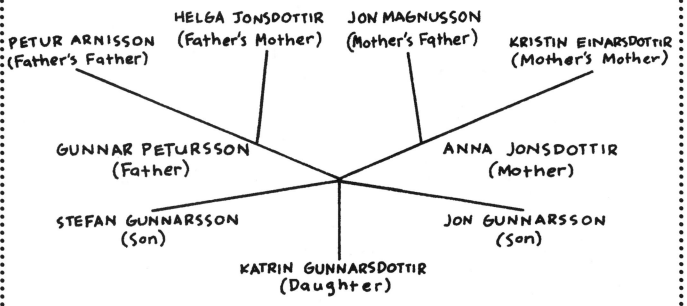

In the figure below, fill in your family's names the way they would be in Iceland.

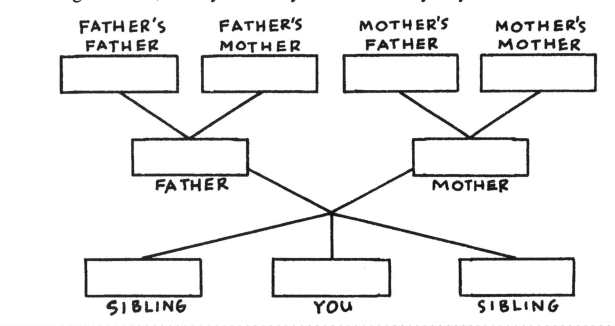

HOMETOWN RESEARCH PACK

Display a map showing the town in which your school is located. Encourage students to make comments about the town or city. Is it big? Small? Crowded? What is the population? Can they count how many parks there are? How many schools? What forms of transportation are used in the town? Where is the library located? Where is the main business district?

Inform students that they can find the answers to these questions by doing research in the local library, city or town hall, and newspaper office, and by asking their parents and local officials.

Create a research packet with the students. It should include some or all of the following information:

> when and how the town was formed
> what the original name was and what the current name is (if applicable)
> who the original occupants were
> who the current occupants are
> total population
> historical facts or events associated with the town or city
> town or city landmarks or preservation spots
> kinds of transportation used when the town was founded and what is used today

Encourage students to think of creative ways in which to present their research. For example, students may wish to make time lines, produce videos showing important historical events in the town, create costumes showing clothing worn by townspeople when the town was first founded, make up dialogues featuring townspeople or founders discussing different aspects of the town, or construct book jackets with front and back covers filled with information.

If desired, hold an assembly for upper grades in which the class may share their information with other classes. Students may also wish to coordinate their efforts and put on a play illustrating the history of the town.

Notable Names Quilt

MATERIALS:

one twin-sized flat bed sheet
fabric crayons or paints and paintbrushes
stapler

DIRECTIONS:

1. Use fabric crayons or paint to divide a twin-sized flat bed sheet into squares, one for each student.
2. Inform students that they will be making an explorers' quilt. Each student will create his or her own design in one of the squares.
3. Direct each child to think of an explorer he or she admires or one with whom he or she would have liked to travel.
4. Invite three or four students at a time to design their squares. Tell students that each square should include the explorer's name, his or her form of transportation, and/or a scene from one of his or her adventures. Each child may also write a sentence telling why he or she likes the chosen explorer. Be sure students sign their names on their squares.
5. Ask volunteers to create pictures for any empty squares.
6. Attach the "quilt" to a wall or bulletin board.
7. You may wish to back the sheet with another sheet of the same size and sew some batting (fluffy filling material used inside quilts) between the two layers. Make more quilts throughout the year on various topics. At the end of the year, each student may have one quilt to take home.

Exploration Quiz

Name _____

Read the information below. Fill in the lines after each sentence with the appropriate event, date, or name. Consult history books or encyclopedias if you need help.

Information Box

1. In 1415 this man began what is known as the "Age of Exploration." He financed trips to explore the west coast of Africa. (name) _____

2. In what century did Marco Polo travel the entire length of the Silk Road, which is about 4,300 miles long? (century) _____

3. Sacajawea, a Native American, guided Meriwether Lewis and William Clark in their exploration of the Northwest Territories in North America. (year) _____

4. Neil Armstrong was the first to do this, in 1969. (event) _____

5. In 1932 this American pilot became the first woman to fly solo across the Atlantic Ocean. (name) _____

6. Roald Amundsen, a Norwegian explorer, reached the South Pole. (year) _____

7. Mary Kingsley, an Englishwoman, went to West Africa to collect river fish and discover new animals. (year) _____

8. Soviet cosmonaut Svetlana Savitskaya became the first woman to walk in space. (year) _____

9. In 1001, Leif Ericson left Greenland to search for land to the southwest. (name of land) _____

10. Around 1490 B.C., this queen sent ships out through the Red Sea and possibly into the Indian Ocean. They found what was probably Somalia, East Africa, where they discovered much ivory, ebony, and myrrh trees.

(name) _____

Exploration Time Line

Name _____

Write in the letter of each item in the appropriate space on the time line below. If necessary, use an encyclopedia or history books for reference.

A. Sir Francis Drake sails around the world.
B. Columbus lands in the West Indies.
C. Marco Polo sets off for China.
D. Roald Amundsen reaches the South Pole.
E. Marquette and Jolliet explore the Mississippi.
F. Magellan sets off to circumnavigate the globe.
G. Vitus Bering sails across the strait between Russia and Alaska.
H. Bartholomeu Dias sails around the Cape of Good Hope.
I. Henry Hudson reaches Hudson Bay.
J. Eric the Red discovers Greenland.

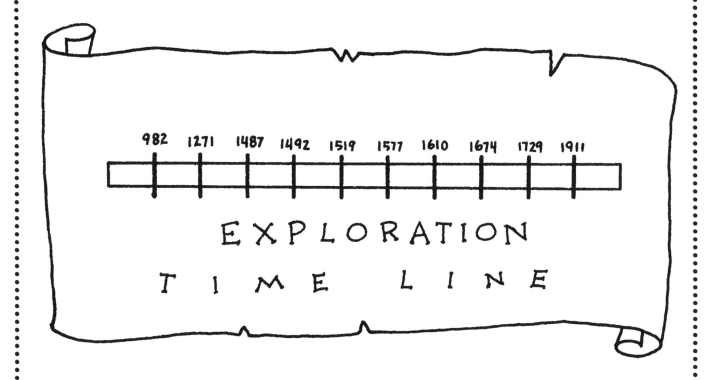

982 1271 1487 1492 1519 1577 1610 1674 1729 1911

EXPLORATION

TIME LINE

Boat Contest

MATERIALS:

Styrofoam peanuts and trays   clay
aluminum foil   wood scraps
construction paper   waxed paper
dough   cups
paper plates   foil pie plates and pans
fabric scraps   large containers of water
old towels

DIRECTIONS:

1. Lay out Styrofoam peanuts and trays, clay, aluminum foil, wood scraps, construction paper, waxed paper, dough, cups, paper plates, foil pie plates and pans, and fabric scraps on several tables.

2. Divide the class into small groups of four to five students each. Give each group a large container of water. Place a towel under each container to absorb any splashed water.

3. Encourage students to experiment to see which materials float and which ones sink. Ask them to jot down notes about each material they test for discussion after the experiments. Encourage students to fold, bend, and crumple the materials to see if the different forms will have any effect.

4. After the class has had enough time to experiment, gather everyone together to discuss the findings. Graph their data.

5. Based on the information in the graph, ask volunteers to tell which materials would make a good boat. Then inform the class that each group will be making a boat of its own.

6. Allow each group plenty of time to plan a design for their boat and write up a list of materials they will need. Try to give the class some free time each day to work on their boats.

7. When the boats are done, ask students to display their work and explain the process they used to make their boats. They should give the names of their boats and explain how the boats move in water.

8. Hold a contest to see which boats are the most seaworthy. Place all the boats in water and time how long each boat stays afloat. If too many contenders are left, try to see which boat can hold the most pennies.

Future Explorers' Club

MATERIALS:

    small boxes and containers
    collage materials
    glue
    paper
    scissors
    clean garbage (ribbons, cans, wheels,
      stuffed toy)
    yarn and/or thread

DIRECTIONS:

1. Explain to the class that they will be forming a club called the Future Explorers' Club. As part of the first meeting, each student should think about a place he or she would like to explore. It may be on land, over ocean, in the ocean, in outer space, in the air, underground, or anywhere else they can imagine. Ask students to share with the club where they would like to go and why.

2. At the next meeting, ask members what types of tools they would need on their trip and what type of clothing and food they would bring. Encourage students to help each other identify necessary items for their trips.

3. At the third meeting, ask students how they would travel to their chosen destinations. Arrange on tables collage materials, clean used containers and recyclables, and yarn or thread for the class to use to create their vehicles. Allow students some time to think about what their forms of transportation will look like and how they will operate.

4. When the vehicles have been completed, have each student write a paragraph describing the purpose, the capacity, and the means of movement of his or her vehicle. Ask each child what type of energy is needed for his or her vehicle to move. Encourage students to add to their paragraphs any other information that they think is important for people to know about their creations.

5. Display the vehicles. Allow time for students to browse through them and read the attached paragraphs. Hold a question-and-answer session afterward for those wanting to comment on classmates' creations.

Exploring Nature

Brainstorm with the class on how explorers, long ago and in modern times, use nature to help them on their expeditions. Encourage students to stretch their imaginations and include in their discussion all areas of exploration and as much of the natural world as they can. List students' ideas on the chalkboard or on a large sheet of paper displayed so that the class can see it.

After all students' ideas have been listed discuss the categories of comments. Decide which might work and which would not work and the reasons why.

Share the following information with the class on explorers and the ways they used nature. Early sea explorers did not travel very far from land. Instead, they used the coastlines to mark their paths. As the desire for trade grew, so too did the paths of voyages. Expeditions would travel out far into the ocean, trying to discover new and exciting places. For these voyages, with no known landmarks in sight, sailors would use the stars to navigate their way.

Explain to the class that these explorers knew that certain stars always stayed in a certain part of the sky in particular times of the year. They knew the sun rose in the east and set in the west. Crews would make use of their information to chart out and check their courses.

Sailors also took advantage of wind currents to help move ships faster along their routes. The route usually taken by early Portuguese explorers on their way to India for purposes of trade was to hug the coastline of west Africa, round the Cape of Good Hope, then sail up the east coast and across to India through the Indian Ocean. On his voyage to India, from 1497 to 1498, Vasco da Gama chose not to follow the usual route. He sailed from Portugal to the Cape Verde Islands. Instead of following the coast, he veered out westward and south into the Atlantic Ocean. There he took advantage of the prevailing winds, and his course turned out to be faster than the old way.

Tell the class that new technology has helped explorers tremendously. When sailors stored food for their voyages, meats and fruits rotted quickly. Meat was usually salted and stored in barrels. Hardtack, a form of biscuit that kept for years, was also brought along on voyages. Now, when astronauts travel into space, their food is dehydrated and keeps for their whole voyage.

Ask students to think of other ways explorers might have used nature in their travels, whether by land, sea, or air: weather, natural dyes, landmarks, food.

Rocket Races

MATERIALS:
>different-sized balloons
>straws
>tape
>different-colored pens
>string

DIRECTIONS:

1. Ask students to predict what will happen when a balloon filled with air is released. Which direction will it take? How far will it go? How fast will it release its air? Will smaller balloons behave differently than bigger balloons?

2. Hand out balloons of different sizes to the class and tell them to blow them up carefully and pinch the opening closed. Then compare and contrast the results of the experiments with the students' predictions.

3. Describe the similarities between rocket propulsion and the energy released by the balloons. (The energy thrusts the object forward). Inform the class that they will be making balloon rockets and having races to see what types of balloons will go the fastest. Distribute the balloons to the class, making sure to hand out several different sizes.

4. Demonstrate how to blow up the balloon partway and tape a straw to a side while keeping the opening closed. Then demonstrate how gently to draw a picture on the balloon to make it resemble a rocket—windows, decals, wings. Allow plenty of time for this part of the assembly.

5. Tie one end of a length of string to a chair back or table leg. Leave the other end free. Repeat the procedure until all students have a string attached to a piece of furniture or taped to the wall. Show students how to blow up their balloons and thread the free end of the string into the straw. Then straighten out the string and release the balloon. Ask students to make observations as they repeat the experiments.

6. Perform the experiments using different sizes of balloons, varying degrees of inflation, and different string lengths. The experiments can also be done to see how the rocket will react to a downward slope of string and an uphill one. Tie a length of string long enough to go across the room and see how far across the room a balloon will go. Which balloons hold enough air to make the journey? Which do not?

17

Naturalist's Journal

Name

A famous naturalist aboard a ship has dropped his journal. The sailors tried to help him put it back together, but all the entries are jumbled.

Help the naturalist identify the animals and write the proper name in its category.

Air	Sea	Land
_____	_____	_____
_____	_____	_____
_____	_____	_____
_____	_____	_____
_____	_____	_____
_____	_____	_____
_____	_____	_____
_____	_____	_____

- a large jumping marsupial (animal with a pouch on front to hold offspring)
- a very large four-legged creature with big ears, a long trunk, and tusks
- a fish that fills itself with water and looks like a spiked balloon
- extremely tall four-legged animal, with long neck, stout body, and long legs, eats tree vegetation
- small-toothed, warm-blooded whales, communicate with one another by making a variety of different sounds
- feathered bird, covered in black with a white front, has wings but does not fly, lives in cold regions of world, good swimmers and divers
- small winged insect, antennae, six legs, great colorful wings, emerges from chrysalis fully grown
- black and white furred animal, two feet and two paws with claws, favorite food is bamboo
- insect that gathers nectar from flowers, lives in a colony
- long animal with no legs; moves by propelling itself with a wiggling motion; eats small animals by swallowing them whole; when danger is near, shakes its tail to warn off possible predators

Hooker's Bag

Name _____

Sir Joseph Hooker was a botanist and explorer of the mid-to-late 19th century. He studied plant life in Antarctica as well as parts of Asia, where he also found many new specimens.

Identify the plants Hooker collected in his bag by reading the descriptions on the next page and writing the names next to the matching pictures of plants. (If a plant is not listed on the identification sheet, you must identify it on your own!)

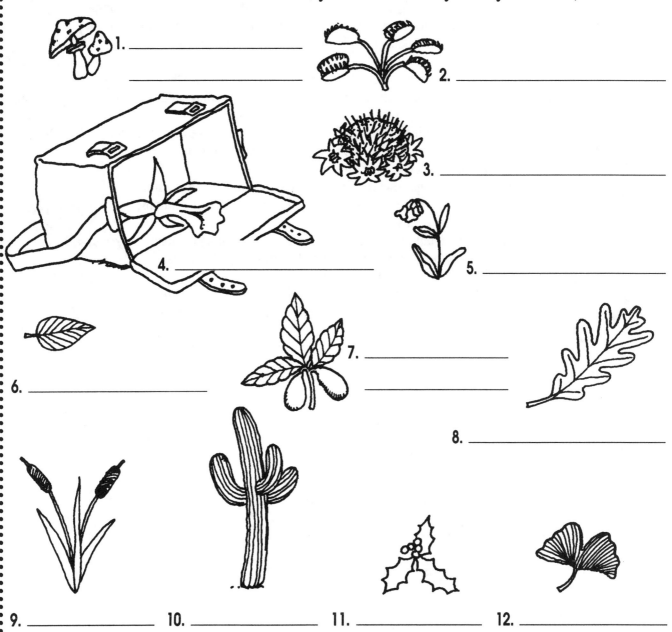

1. _____

2. _____

3. _____

4. _____

5. _____

6. _____

7. _____

8. _____

9. _____ 10. _____ 11. _____ 12. _____

Hooker's Plants

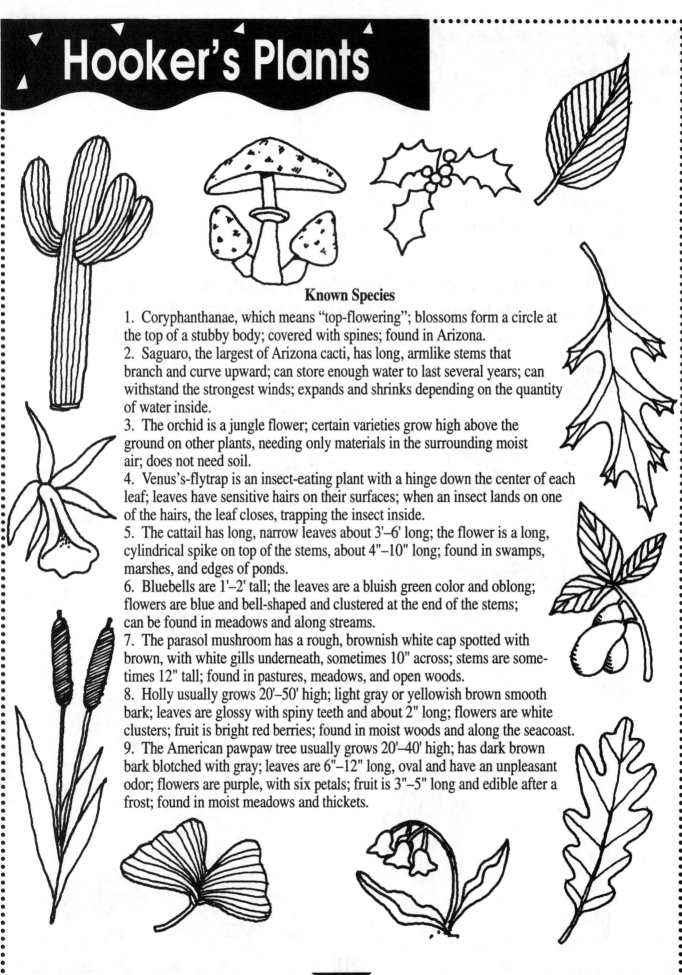

Known Species

1. Coryphanthanae, which means "top-flowering"; blossoms form a circle at the top of a stubby body; covered with spines; found in Arizona.

2. Saguaro, the largest of Arizona cacti, has long, armlike stems that branch and curve upward; can store enough water to last several years; can withstand the strongest winds; expands and shrinks depending on the quantity of water inside.

3. The orchid is a jungle flower; certain varieties grow high above the ground on other plants, needing only materials in the surrounding moist air; does not need soil.

4. Venus's-flytrap is an insect-eating plant with a hinge down the center of each leaf; leaves have sensitive hairs on their surfaces; when an insect lands on one of the hairs, the leaf closes, trapping the insect inside.

5. The cattail has long, narrow leaves about 3'–6' long; the flower is a long, cylindrical spike on top of the stems, about 4"–10" long; found in swamps, marshes, and edges of ponds.

6. Bluebells are 1'–2' tall; the leaves are a bluish green color and oblong; flowers are blue and bell-shaped and clustered at the end of the stems; can be found in meadows and along streams.

7. The parasol mushroom has a rough, brownish white cap spotted with brown, with white gills underneath, sometimes 10" across; stems are sometimes 12" tall; found in pastures, meadows, and open woods.

8. Holly usually grows 20'–50' high; light gray or yellowish brown smooth bark; leaves are glossy with spiny teeth and about 2" long; flowers are white clusters; fruit is bright red berries; found in moist woods and along the seacoast.

9. The American pawpaw tree usually grows 20'–40' high; has dark brown bark blotched with gray; leaves are 6"–12" long, oval and have an unpleasant odor; flowers are purple, with six petals; fruit is 3"–5" long and edible after a frost; found in moist meadows and thickets.

20

Water Pressure Experiments

MATERIALS:
different-sized tin cans
large nails
hammers
large buckets

DIRECTIONS:

1. Explain to the class that deep-sea exploration was not possible until this century because the deeper a diver went, the more pressure the water exerted on his or her body. A bathyscaphe, a boat capable of withstanding water pressure at great depths, was invented by Auguste Piccard and his son Jacques in the mid-20th century. Jacques took it down to 7 miles below sea level in 1960. Since then deep-sea exploration has become more common, and we are learning more and more about life under the sea.

2. Inform the class that they will be doing experiments that will help them understand water pressure more clearly. Divide the class into groups of three and give each group a can, a large nail, and a hammer. Demonstrate how to hammer the nail through three areas on a can—high up, in the middle, and near the bottom. Tell the groups that each member will make a hole in their can. A team member should hold the can steady while the holes are made.

3. Over a water table or sink, have two members place their fingers over the holes while the third mem-

ber fills the can with water. Have the two team members remove their fingers at the count of three. Ask students to jot down their observations.

4. When all groups have had a chance to observe the experiment, gather the class together and compare notes. Ask students to explain why the hole nearest the bottom had the longest spurt. (The pressure exerted on the water nearest the bottom was the greatest.)

5. Next, distribute a bucket to each group. Ask one member to fill the bucket. Then demonstrate to the class how to place one hand palm up in the water at the bottom of the bucket. Drag the hand up as quickly as possible. Then repeat with the hand held near the top of the water in the bucket.

6. Ask each group to repeat the procedure until everyone has had a turn dragging his or her hand to the surface of the water. Which was easier, deeper water or shallow water? Why do they think it was harder to bring their hand to the surface when it was at the bottom of the bucket? (Again, the water pressure was greater at the bottom.)

Math Explorations

Name

Connect the dots from the smallest number to the largest to see what form of transportation this explorer wants to use.

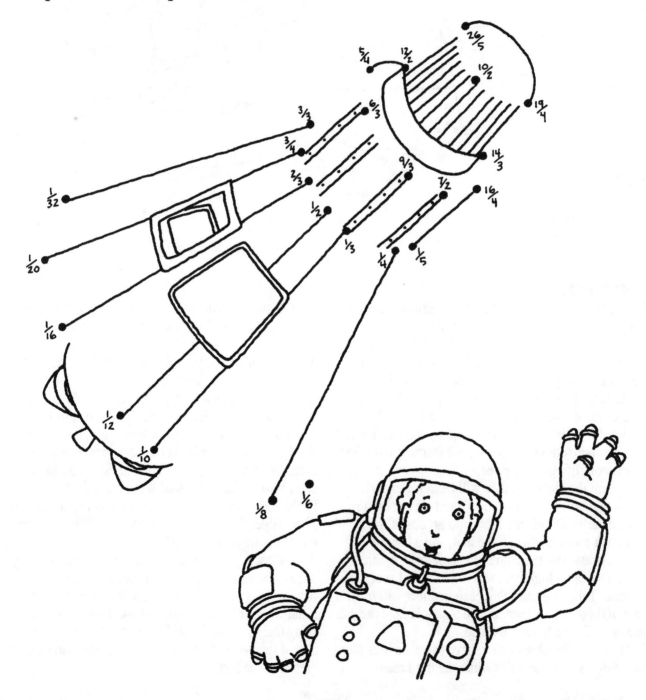

Ship's Inventory

SHOPPING LIST
1. ONIONS
2. DRIED BEANS
3. CHEESE
4. FISH
5. FLOUR

Name _____

Pretend that you are the captain of a sailing ship that is about to take a two-month voyage. Circle the supplies you think it will be necessary to have on board. There will be 20 people on your crew, and you do not know when you will be able to purchase fresh supplies. Next to each item, write how many units you think you will need. Then total the cost for each item. Finally, add up the cost of your entire list.

On the back of this page, write a letter to your sponsor stating your reasons for including the supplies you chose.

Item	Quantity	Price	Amount needed	Cost
Onions	1-pound bag	$1.69	_____	_____
Dried beans	12 bags	$7.20	_____	_____
Salted meat	1 barrel	$25.00	_____	_____
Salted fish	1 barrel	$19.50	_____	_____
Cheese	6 bricks	$8.75	_____	_____
Ship biscuit	5-pound bag	$10.99	_____	_____
Log books	dozen	$3.00	_____	_____
Water	1 barrel	$15.00	_____	_____
Flour	5-pound bag	$2.00	_____	_____
Sugar	5-pound bag	$3.50	_____	_____
Oil	2-liter bottle	$1.75	_____	_____
Bacon	3 pounds	$10.00	_____	_____
First-aid kit	1	$40.00	_____	_____
Sailcloth	1 yard	$3.99	_____	_____
Thread	1 spool	$0.69	_____	_____
Rope	25 feet	$16.00	_____	_____
Lifeboat	1	$345.00	_____	_____
Crew uniform	1	$55.32	_____	_____
Books	1	$6.99	_____	_____
Stereo system	1	$168.45	_____	_____
Cassettes	1	$4.89	_____	_____

A Fair Trade

Name _____

Use the code box to work out the problems below. Choose three problems and explain how you solved them. Write your explanations on the back of the worksheet.

Code Box

1 yard of silk = 2 ounces of gold
10 ounces of gold = 1-pound bag of spices
1 beaver pelt = 5 ounces of ivory
1 small piece of porcelain pottery = 3 pieces of silver
glass-bead necklace = silver bowl
12 ounces of ivory = sled
10 pieces of silver = 20 pieces of gold
6 ounces of gold = 1 gold piece

---

1. You have been out trapping for a month. On your sled are 50 beaver pelts. How many ounces of ivory can you get? How many pounds? _____

2. A trader comes to the station with 30 ounces of gold. He wants to trade for some silk. He insists his total comes to 13 yards of silk. Is he right? If not, what is his total yardage?

_____

3. A merchant in India is selling spices in exchange for silver. He wants 15 pieces of silver for 1 bag of cinnamon. You do not have silver, but you do have six pieces of porcelain pottery. How many bags of cinnamon can you get with your porcelain? Will there be any porcelain left over?

_____

4. As a gift to your mother, you buy two glass-bead necklaces. How much did you have to pay for the gift? _____

5. If a silver bowl were melted down, it would yield 40 silver pieces. How much porcelain pottery could you buy? _____

6. Your friend has 55 gold pieces. She wants to buy some spices. How can she do it? How many bags of spices can she get? Will she have any gold left over? _____

_____

Roman Inventory

Name

Read the inventory of items in this Roman store. Then rewrite the Roman numerals, using their Arabic numeral equivalents. Represent each number on the abacus with the matching letter. The first one has been done for you.

Inventory

a. LII pairs of sandals

b. CLXXVIII tunics

c. IV gold belts

d. CCXCIX fabric belts

e. MCCV wigs

f. DCC gold armbands

g. LXV makeup kits

h. MMDCCCXLIII pitcher and cup sets

i. IX silver plates

a.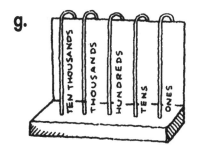

b.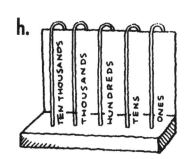

c.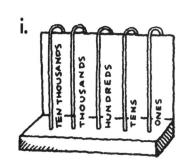

d.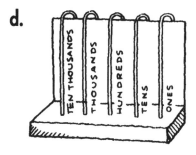

e.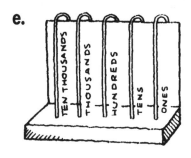

f.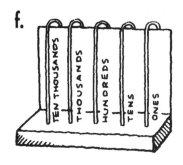

g.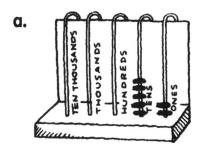

h.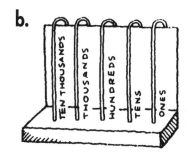

i.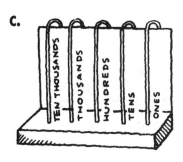

Temperature Changes Graph

Name _____

Read the table about summer temperatures on page 27. Then use a world map to research the latitude of each city. Convert the information from the table and the world map onto the graph. (You may wish to use a different color for each mark on the graph, or you may label the marks with the city and country's initials.)

The first one has been done for you.

Use the information on the graph to answer the questions on the next page.

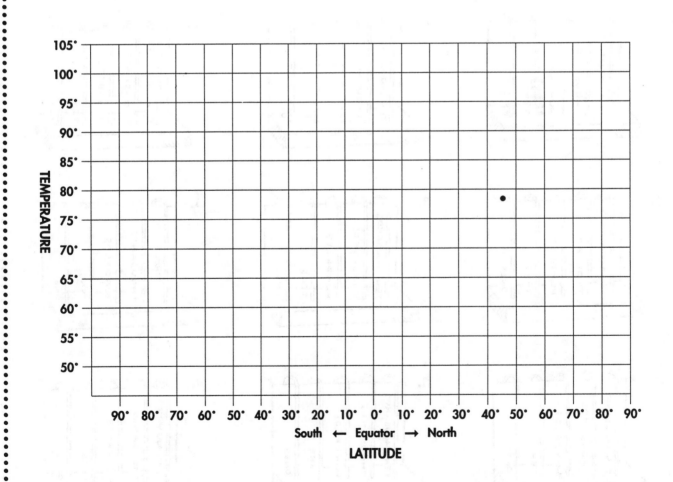

Temperature Changes Graph

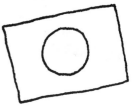
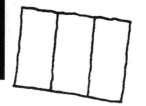
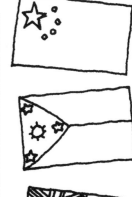

Name

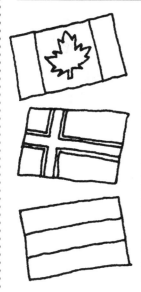

Location	Temperature	Latitude
Montreal, Canada	78° F	46° N
Moscow, Russia	76° F	_____
Reykjavik, Iceland	58° F	_____
Tehran, Iran	99° F	_____
Sydney, Australia	60° F	_____
Manila, Philippines	88° F	_____
Shanghai, China	91° F	_____
Tokyo, Japan	83° F	_____
Dublin, Ireland	67° F	_____
La Paz, Bolivia	62° F	_____

1. Which two cities have approximately the same latitude in degrees but are on opposite sides of the equator? _____

2. Which two cities have one of the smallest difference in degrees temperature but the largest difference in degrees latitude? What are the differences? _____

_____

3. Which two cities have an approximate difference in degrees latitude that is the same as the square root of 25? _____

4. Which two cities are the closest (approximately) in degrees latitude but have reversed digits in degrees temperature? _____

5. Why do you think Reykjavik has the coolest summer temperature? _____

_____

6. How many cities have degree latitude South? Which ones? _____

_____

7. What is the approximate difference in degrees latitude between Manila and Reykjavik?

_____

8. What is the sum of degrees latitude for the three warmest cities? _____

_____

Stargazers

Early explorers depended on the stars to guide them on their voyages. On the lines provided, identify each of the constellations below and tell where in the sky it is located. Consult a reference book on astronomy or an encyclopedia if you need help.

1. _____

_____

2. _____

_____

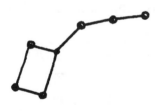

3. _____

_____

4. _____

_____

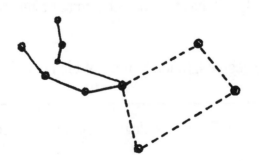

5. _____

_____

Outer Space Explorations

Name _____

Answer the questions below based on the information given in the table.

Location	Distance from sun	Time needed for one orbit around sun	Size
Mercury	36 million miles	88 days	3,000 miles diameter
Venus	67 million miles	225 days	7,500 miles diameter
Mars	141.5 million miles	687 days	4,200 miles diameter
Jupiter	483 million miles	12 yrs	88,900 miles diameter
Saturn	885 million miles	29.5 yrs	74,900 miles diameter
Uranus	1.8 billion miles	84 yrs	31,800 miles diameter
Neptune	2.8 billion miles	165 yrs	30,800 miles diameter
Pluto	3.7 billion miles	248 yrs	1,400 miles diameter
Earth	93 million miles	365 days	7,900 miles diameter

1. Order the planets from smallest to largest. _____

_____

_____

2. Order the planets from closest to the sun to farthest away. _____

_____

_____

3. How many days does it take Jupiter to orbit around the sun? _____

_____

4. Which planet takes 1/7 the time it takes Uranus to orbit the sun? _____

5. If the planets were in line from the sun, how far would it be to go from Mercury to Venus? From

Jupiter to Saturn? From Earth to Pluto? _____

_____

Flight Distance

Name

Name
_____

Answer the questions on page 31 based on the information given in the map.

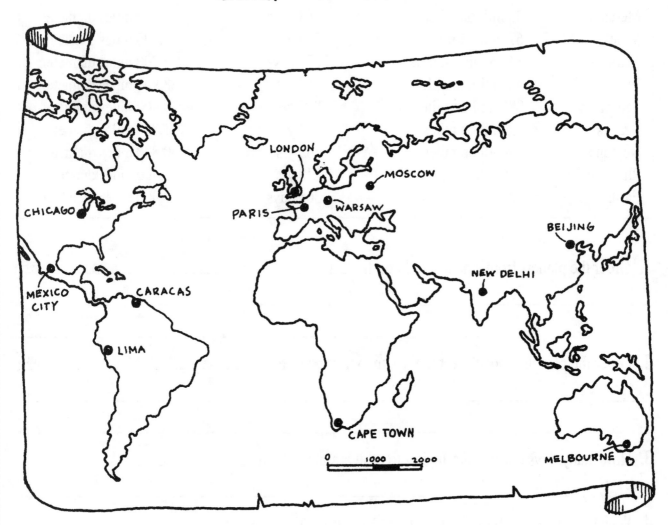

½ INCH = 1000 MILES

Flight Distance

Name _____

1. Approximately how many miles is it from Beijing to Caracas? _____

2. If you were flying from London to Moscow and could carry only enough fuel to travel 1,000 miles, where might you stop to refuel? _____

3. Which is farther to fly, Melbourne to Cape Town, or London to Cape Town? _____
_____

4. You find flying rather exhausting and want to make a leisurely trip from Mexico City to New Delhi. Suppose you plan on stopping every 3,000 miles. Approximately how many days will it take you to get to New Delhi? _____

5. A friend wants to tour the highlighted cities in the Americas and has asked you to plan the trip. You want to take the most direct route possible to save on fuel. If you were picking her up in Chicago and ending in Lima, what would be the order of your trip and approximately how many total miles would you be flying? _____
_____

6. Which is the shorter distance, Melbourne to Caracas or Melbourne to Chicago? _____
_____

7. Approximately how many miles is it from Moscow to Melbourne? _____

8. You are going to visit your grandparents in Beijing. You begin your journey in London, stop in Paris, then fly on to Beijing. Approximately how long is the journey? _____

9. Which is the longer distance, Lima to Moscow or Lima to New Delhi? _____
_____

10. You are taking a world tour. You fly from Paris to Warsaw; Warsaw to Moscow; Moscow to Beijing; Beijing to Melbourne; Melbourne to Chicago; Chicago to London. Approximately how many miles will you travel altogether? _____

Spelunking Discoveries

Name _____

You are spelunking in an unexplored cave. Solve each of the problems below and find the answers in the number square—up, down, backward, forward, or diagonally. Each answer will spell a word to tell you what you will find in the caves.

1. 5,256 divided by 8 _____

2. 635 x 7 _____

3. 10 to the third power _____

4. 10,137,586,001 + 864,003,297 _____

5. 4,444 - 2,555 _____

6. 67,800 divided by 5 _____

7. 75% of 500 _____

8. 67 squared _____

9 Y	5 U	3 O	1 B	9 Z	6 F	2 U	5 R	7 T	0 O	8 S	7 C
6 L	0 R	4 W	6 L	8 A	3 B	1 T	4 S	9 E	9 E	6 L	5 R
2 A	7 W	4 I	9 L	5 R	8 T	1 J	0 H	2 T	1 K	7 B	3 Y
1 G	5 O	4 L	4 I	8 M	9 E	9 S	9 I	5 A	8 G	3 T	0 S
0 M	4 Z	5 L	7 B	2 O	1 A	8 M	7 P	9 D	4 E	0 S	8 T
9 I	0 D	3 N	0 I	6 M	5 G	4 E	3 T	2 R	6 H	1 F	6 A
5 T	0 N	2 W	3 C	1 A	0 H	2 W	6 Y	5 O	7 U	2 W	4 L
6 S	0 I	5 G	0 L	6 C	9 F	7 X	4 T	2 M	3 O	5 S	3 S
3 A	1 F	0 A	4 K	5 D	1 L	3 A	5 K	6 E	0 S	0 U	6 C
2 O	1 T	6 S	7 E	0 A	7 K	7 N	6 V	5 X	3 D	1 T	9 O
1 S	9 T	7 A	8 L	6 A	2 G	5 D	9 N	4 F	2 I	7 M	8 R

Trading Station

Name

Answer the questions based on the information given on the sign at the trading station.

TRADING STATION

1 BEAVER PELT = 15 SILVER COINS
1 BEAR SKIN = 30 SILVER COINS
5 SILVER COINS = 1 GOLD COIN

1. Trapper Tim comes into the station with 50 beaver pelts. He would like to get gold for his pelts. How much will he get? _____

2. Outdoors Ozzie steps up to the counter claiming he has double the number of pelts Tim brought in. How much will he get in silver coins? Gold coins? _____

3. Grizzly Gus brings in a bag of gold coins and wants to trade them for silver. He is planning on melting the silver down and making some jewelry for the tourist trade. How much silver will he get if one bag contains 25 gold coins? _____

4. Mountain Man arrives around midday to buy supplies for the next month. He will need flour, eggs, sugar, honey, and beans. The total will be seven gold coins. How many bear skins will he need to trade to get his supplies? _____

5. Hearty Hannah steps in the station to visit the proprietor and trade in eggs for bear skins. She would like to make bear skin blankets for her four children. Each blanket will require 1 1/2 skins. How many eggs will she need to give if each skin costs 75 eggs? _____

6. If Hannah brings in 25 eggs a week, how much time will it take her to raise the amount she needs? Convert the time into days and months. _____

7. If it is July when she starts her trading, will she have the skins in time for the first snowfall in the beginning of December? _____

8. Fresh Air Freddy's sled can hold 128 beaver pelts and 80 bear skins when fully loaded. If the sled is 3/4 full, how many pelts and skins are on it? _____

Commemorative Stamps

MATERIALS:

crayons or markers
construction paper
scissors
collage materials
glue

DIRECTIONS:

1. Inform the class that stamps are sometimes used to commemorate people who have contributed something to their countries, their cultures, and the lives of those around them.

2. Ask each student to think of the explorer he or she feels has contributed the most to the knowledge we now have of the world in which we live. Encourage students to share their choices with the class.

3. Have the children write mock letters to the postmaster general explaining why stamps should be made to commemorate their chosen explorers. Be sure students use the proper form for writing business letters.

4. Distribute crayons or markers, paper, scissors, collage materials, and glue to the students and ask them to design a stamp to honor their chosen explorer.

5. Attach the letters to the respective stamps and display them on a wall or a bulletin board. Invite other classes to come and view the display. Place a comment box near the display so visitors can add their opinions about who they feel was (or is) an important explorer. Discuss their suggestions in class.

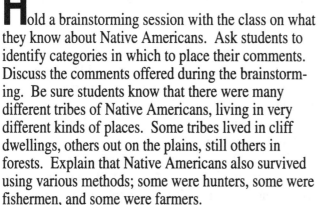

Hold a brainstorming session with the class on what they know about Native Americans. Ask students to identify categories in which to place their comments. Discuss the comments offered during the brainstorming. Be sure students know that there were many different tribes of Native Americans, living in very different kinds of places. Some tribes lived in cliff dwellings, others out on the plains, still others in forests. Explain that Native Americans also survived using various methods; some were hunters, some were fishermen, and some were farmers.

Tell students that when European explorers first came to North America, Native Americans had already been living on that land for thousands of years. The explorers and subsequent settlers claimed native lands for themselves. This angered native peoples, who did not believe that anyone could "own" the land. The government began to set aside certain areas in which Native Americans were to reside. Point out that many tribes are now trying to regain parts of their ancestral land from the government, and some are winning their cases in court.

Encourage students to check the local library to find out if their area is one in which Native Americans originally lived or still live. Have students try to find out what tribes lived there, what languages these Native Americans spoke, what they ate, what kind of houses they lived in, what kind of clothes they wore, and what kinds of toys the children had. Bring in books about Native American life for students to look at. Set aside time each day for students' investigations into these topics.

Inform the class that they will be making models of different kinds of homes resembling those made by the Native Americans. Share with the class books from the library emphasizing the many different styles of homes Native Americans built: pueblos, tepees, long-houses, hogans, cliff dwellings, and the early pit houses. Divide the class into groups depending on what type of house they would like to build. Set aside time for group meetings during which the students will decide on materials to use, what base to use, how to decorate the model and its surroundings to make them look realistic, and who will do each part of the project.

When the groups have completed their homes, allow the students to browse among them. Afterward, hold a meeting in which groups will present to the class their information on a typical day in the life of their chosen tribe and explain their home. Encourage the class to make comments, ask questions, and make suggestions.

35

Explorer Float

MATERIALS:

shoe boxes
construction paper
scissors
glue
fabric scraps

shirt boxes
crayons or markers
collage materials
tape
oaktag

DIRECTIONS:

1. Inform the class that they will be constructing floats for an Explorer's Parade. The floats will be made with a box base, which can be as small or large as is reasonably possible. Distribute shoe boxes and shirt boxes to the class, along with construction paper, crayons or markers, scissors, collage materials, glue, tape, fabric scraps, and oaktag.

2. Before students make their floats, ask each child to choose an explorer to be the subject of his or her project. Students should go to the library to find information on their explorers. Encourage the children to try to find pictures of what their explorers looked (or look) like.

3. Students' floats may show a scene from one of their explorer's adventures, a likeness of their explorer, a futuristic version of what their explorer may have done had he or she lived into our time period, or an imaginary scene (for example, Jacques Cousteau exploring the moon).

4. When the floats are finished, have students line them up around the room. Ask each child to write a brief paragraph about his or her explorer and what the floats tell about that explorer.

5. Invite other classes in to view the parade. Display the parade in a case in the hallway where the whole school as well as visitors may see and enjoy it.

Ship Building

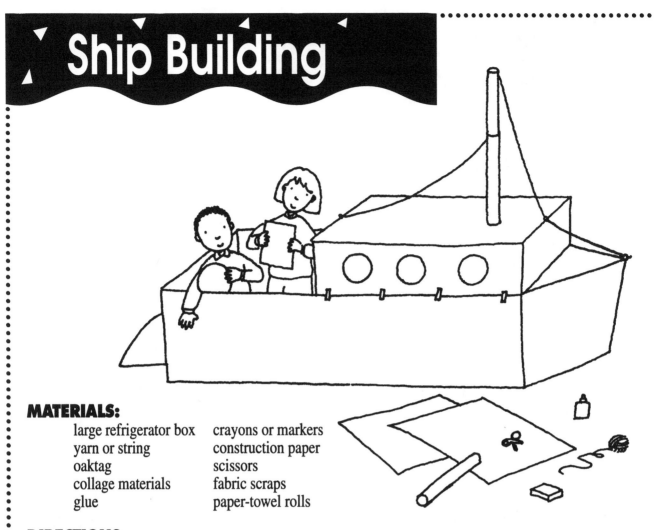

MATERIALS:

large refrigerator box   crayons or markers
yarn or string   construction paper
oaktag   scissors
collage materials   fabric scraps
glue   paper-towel rolls

DIRECTIONS:

1. Borrow books from the library about ships and how they are constructed. Share these books with the class.
2. Encourage students to learn the proper words for the various parts of the ships. Give the class a description for a part of a ship and ask volunteers to tell you the name of it, or let students give descriptions and have classmates guess the name.
3. Ship vocabulary to use with the class includes:

mainmast	mizzenmast
foremast	bowsprit
stern	bow
starboard	sail
cargo	lifeboat
rudder	anchor
main deck	cabins
tiller	ship's stores

4. Discuss the crew members who might be aboard these ships: captain, surgeon, first mate, steward, sailmakers, cook, soldiers, carpenters, coopers, caulkers, ordinary seamen, and ship's boys.
5. Distribute the materials students will need to decorate their ship models. Parts of the ship, such as windows or rudder, may be made using construction paper or oaktag. Use yarn or string for the rigging, and paper or fabric scraps to make sails. An anchor can be made from paper-towel rolls by taping them end to end or pushing one halfway into the next until the right length is achieved. An anchor may be attached to a ship using yarn loops tied one inside another to resemble a chain.

6. When the ships are done, see if students have any comments on their projects. Ask them questions, such as:

> Do you think this project was easy or difficult?
> If you had to do it over again, would you have done anything differently?
> What would you like to name the ship?

7. If desired, have a naming ceremony and toast the ship with apple cider.
8. You may wish to donate the ship to a younger grade for dramatic play. Students may explain the parts of the ship to the younger students and show them where everything belongs.

A Work of Art

Divide the class into groups of four. Give each group a 12" x 18" piece of white paper. Demonstrate how to fold the paper into fourths widthwise and then ask one child in each group to fold the paper.

Explain to the groups that they will be making a group art picture. One person in each group will go first; that student will draw the head and neck of an explorer. Before passing the paper to the second student, who will draw the upper body to the waist, the first artist should fold back his or her section so it cannot be seen.

When they've completed their drawings, the second students should fold their sections back so the third set of artists cannot see their work. Students may leave a few lines to mark where their drawings stopped for the next artist to start from. The third student in each group will draw the portion of the explorer from the waist to the top of the legs. The fourth student will draw the explorer's legs and feet.

When the fourth student in each group is finished, open the drawings. Allow time for the students to view their group effort, then gather the class together. Ask each student in the groups to explain what they were drawing. Did any of the groups have the same explorer in mind? Or did all the students in each group draw a different one?

Display the students' work with an index card attached identifying the artists and explaining what explorers they were thinking of while they were drawing.

Land Ho! Telescope

MATERIALS:

paper-towel rolls
masking tape
construction paper
paints and paintbrushes
scissors
glue
collage materials
yarn

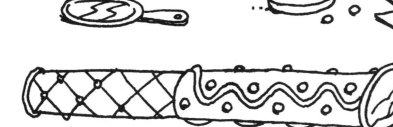

DIRECTIONS:

1. Explain to the class that telescopes were used by travelers to identify landmarks or headlands from great distances and thereby recognize the viewer's position at sea. The telescope was invented at approximately the same time in three countries—Italy, Holland, and England—in the early part of the 17th century.

2. Distribute the materials and inform the class that they will be making telescopes. To form the length of the telescopes, show each child how to crush one end of a paper-towel roll slightly until it fits into the end of another one. Push it in gently, then tape in place.

3. Students may cover their telescopes with construction paper or paint. Collage materials make wonderful decorations on the telescope, especially small, jewellike beads. Yarn may be used to create a pattern around the eye hole or down the sides.

4. If possible, tape a plastic magnifying glass about the same diameter as the paper-towel roll to the end of each telescope to give a more realistic touch.

5. Take the class outside to try out their telescopes. Although they may not be able to see distant objects, the telescopes will help focus their attention on one image at a time.

All Systems Go!

Name _____

Use the answers to the clue questions below to fill in the correct boxes of the puzzle.

Across

1. Before the compass was invented, this naturally magnetic iron oxide was used to tell direction. When hung, it always pointed north.

5. This device was designed to determine latitude but was very inaccurate because it swung too much as a ship moved.

6. The first to make a sea crossing by aircraft, across the English Channel, in 1909.

7. An instrument for showing direction consisting of a magnetic needle swinging on a pivot and pointing to the magnetic north.

9. The most important product traded along the Silk Road.

11. The name of the first satellite to orbit Earth, launched by Russia in 1957.

13. The first man to walk on the moon.

Down

2. This advanced instrument measures latitude to within 0.01 of a degree.

3. The main reason people begin to explore routes to new places.

4. A ship's captain keeps one of these and writes the events of the day in it as well as the length and direction traveled.

7. The other commander of the expedition made by Meriwether Lewis across the Northwest Territories in North America.

8. The object that catches wind and helps move a ship along its way.

10. The person in charge of a ship during its voyage.

12. This object is lowered to the bottom of the water to keep a ship from drifting.

14. A revolt by sailors or soldiers against their officers.

What's in a Name?

For each student in the class, write a different explorer's name on a 9" x 12" piece of construction paper. Tape one name to each student's back, making sure he or she does not see the name. Some suggestions:

Charles Darwin   Henry Bates
Mary Kingsley   Marco Polo
James Cook   Dr. Livingstone
Henry Hudson   Vitus Bering
Amelia Earhart   Amy Johnson
Charles Lindbergh   Prince Henry
Leif Ericson   Cheng Ho
Bartholomeu Dias   Christopher Columbus
Neil Armstrong   Jacques Cousteau
Roald Amundsen   Ibn Batuta

The object of the game is for students to guess whose name is on their backs. To play, each student must ask his or her classmates questions that will help reveal the explorer's name. The questions must be yes-and-no questions.

Each child should continue asking questions until he or she is ready to guess the name of the explorer. If the guess is correct, that student may go back into the game to answer other student's questions. If the guess is incorrect, the student may continue playing the game by asking more yes-and-no questions.

If desired, set a time limit to end the game. For younger students, you may wish to write a list of possible explorers on the chalkboard for them to refer to while playing.

Explorers Press Conference

Miss Kingsley! Miss Kingsley!

What was your most dangerous experience?

PRESS

Read the following excerpts from *The Permanent Book of Explorations*, edited by John Keay and published by Carroll and Graf (1994). Ask students to pretend that they are attending a press conference at which the people quoted in the excerpts are speaking. Tell students to write down questions they would like to ask at the press conference.

1. Mary Kingsley grew up in England. After her elderly parents died, she decided to go to West Africa in 1892 to study fish for the British Museum. The following is an excerpt from her account of adventures along the Ogowe river:

> These narrow shaded swamps gave us a world of trouble and took up a good deal of time. Sometimes the leader of the party would make three or four attempts before he found a ford, going on until the black, batter-like ooze came up round his neck, and then turning back and trying in another place. . . .

2. John Hanning Speke, while returning with Richard Francis Burton from Lake Tanganyika, decided to travel north in search of a bigger lake reported to him by an Arab informant. He later named the lake he found Victoria and declared it the source of the White Nile.

> It is always foolish to travel without an assortment of beads, in consequence of the tastes of the different tribes varying so much; and it is more economical in the long-run to purchase high-priced than low-priced beads when making up the caravan at Zanzibar. . . .

3. Fridtjof Nansen was a Norwegian explorer who almost reached the North Pole in 1895. His party took refuge on an ice floe when they could no longer make their way through the ice-filled water.

> We load our sledges and try to drag them inward towards land, but soon we see that the pace we are drifting at is too much for us. So we begin again to look around us for a safer floe to pitch our camp on, as our present one seems somewhat shaky.

A Letter to a Friend

Ask the class to think about what life might be like for an explorer while away from home on an expedition. Discuss various situations, such as hygiene, food, bad weather, danger, different climates, different cultures, and diseases. Lead the discussion to more pleasant aspects, such as the beauty of their surroundings, the excitement of attaining their goal, meeting new and interesting peoples, learning new languages, and feeling the thrill of the unknown.

Debate the issue of exploration. Did these expeditions benefit the explorers' countries or the native peoples? Discuss such questions as what became of Native Americans after Europeans began settling in North America, and what became of native Hawaiians after explorers began settling in Hawaii.

Dear Marc,
I am writing from Accra on Africa's west coast. My guides and I have made our way through thick forests and along rivers. Yesterday a large crocodile attacked our canoe! I hit it on the nose with my oar and it swam away.
Mary Kingsley

Distribute paper and pens and ask the class to imagine they are explorers and write letters to friends back home. Brainstorm about the items they can include in their letters. Have the students write as different explorers going into the same region and giving their varied viewpoints and experiences. Or, to give more variety to the letters, have the class write about different regions.

When the letters are completed, demonstrate how to mount them on colorful construction paper. Bind the papers into book form and ask some volunteers to design a cover for the book. Share the book with the class, asking each writer to read his or her letter to the class. Then place the book on a shelf in the social studies center so students may read it on their own during free time.

43

Word Box

DOGSLED

Name

_____

Write a word in each category box that begins with the letter in the left column. For each word that you write that no one else has written, you win one point. The person with the most points wins. The sample chart shows each category box filled in.

DENMARK

DARWIN

	Animal	Food	City
D	dinosaur	doughnuts	Denver
E	elephant	eggs	Edinburgh
N	nut hatch	nachos	New York
I	iguana	ice cream	Istanbul
S	snake	sandwich	Seville
E	eel	eggplant	El Paso

	Place	Travelers' Tool	Explorer's Name
D			
I			
S			
C			
O			
V			
E			
R			

Creative Voyages

Name _____

Read the story starters listed below. Then choose one and write a story that begins with that sentence. On a separate piece of paper, draw an illustration to go along with your story.

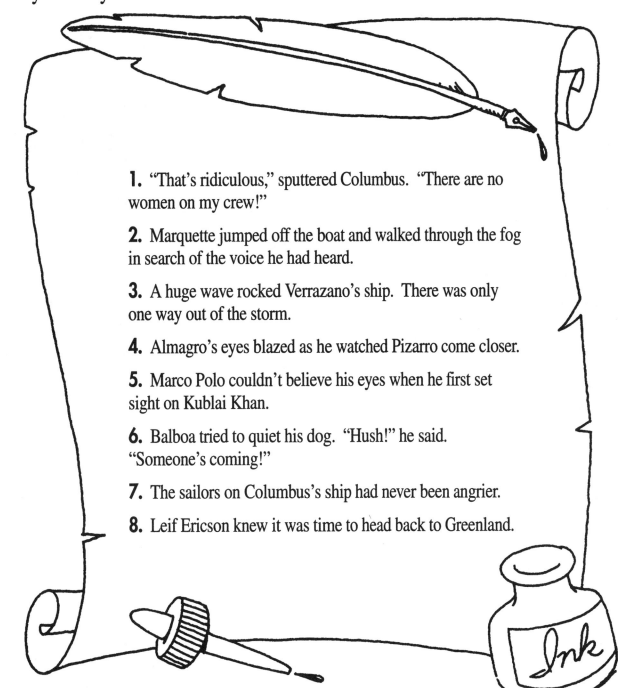

1. "That's ridiculous," sputtered Columbus. "There are no women on my crew!"

2. Marquette jumped off the boat and walked through the fog in search of the voice he had heard.

3. A huge wave rocked Verrazano's ship. There was only one way out of the storm.

4. Almagro's eyes blazed as he watched Pizarro come closer.

5. Marco Polo couldn't believe his eyes when he first set sight on Kublai Khan.

6. Balboa tried to quiet his dog. "Hush!" he said. "Someone's coming!"

7. The sailors on Columbus's ship had never been angrier.

8. Leif Ericson knew it was time to head back to Greenland.

News Travels Quickly

© 1996 Troll Creative Teacher Ideas

Name _____

Printing presses and newspapers did not exist when much of the world's exploration took place. Imagine that they did. Using one of the headlines below, write a news article about an exciting discovery.

_____

_____

_____

_____

_____

_____

_____

_____

_____

_____

_____

_____

_____

Category Cards

DIRECTIONS:

1. Write categories of exploration topics on index cards. Categories may include: food, disease, place names, travelers' tools, weather, danger, culture, climate, shelter, and people. A category may be written on two cards if necessary.

2. Place the cards facedown in a pile in front of the players. The first player calls a letter from the alphabet and then picks the top card off the pile. He or she reads the category written on the card.

3. Players then try to be the first to call out a word that fits both conditions—it begins with the letter called, and it fits in the category named on the card. The first player to call out a correct answer is the next to choose a letter and pick a card from the pile.

4. When a player calls out a right answer, he or she is awarded the category card to keep until the end of the game. The game is over when all the cards have been used. The player with the most cards wins the game.

DANGER

DISEASE

CULTURE

WEATHER

FOOD

PEOPLE

SHELTER...

47

Geography Trail

Gather the class together in a circle. Tell the students they will be playing a game in which they will be naming place names. Point to one student to begin the game. Tell that child to name any place in the world he or she wishes.

The next player, the student sitting to the first player's right, then names a place that begins with the last letter of the previous player's word.

If a student cannot think of a place, he or she is out, and the next student goes. That student must call out a place name that begins with the previous player's word.

You may make the game as easy or challenging as you wish. Instead of taking students out of the game for not thinking up a place name, they may pass and stay in the game. Allow students to name lakes, rivers, mountain ranges, or other geographical locations as well as continents, countries, states, cities, and towns. Or have students name locations on one continent or in one country or one city. You may allow names to be used only once or repeatedly throughout the game.

1. D_R_I_ Sailed a ship called the Beagle.

2. L_N_B_R_H Flew across the Atlantic.

3. C_L_M_U_ Discovered America.

4. C_U_T_A_ Explores under ocean.

5. L_V_N_S_O_E Discovered Victoria Falls.

6. K_N_S_E_ Explored Africa.

7. A_M_T_O-G First man on the moon.

8. E_I_S_N Viking explorer.

9. H_D_O_ English explorer.

10. P_L_ First European to cross Asia.

Give each student a piece of paper and a pen. Ask each child to write out a list of ten explorers' names.

Tell students to cross out every other letter of all the names on their lists, beginning with the second letter in each name. After they have crossed out the letters, ask students to write a short clue about the identity of the explorer next to each name.

Have students switch papers with classmates. Give the class five minutes to try to solve each other's puzzles. When the five minutes are up, see who solved the most names. If desired, allow students more time, or let them continue until everyone is finished.

This game may also be played using place names, forms of transportation, travelers' tools, or any category that fits the current curriculum.

Packing Up

Gather the class together in a circle. Tell students that they will be playing a game about going on a trip. Begin by taking a class vote about where the destination should be. Some suggested locations are the North or South Pole, the Himalayas, the Amazon, and the Sahara.

Inform the class that they will need to pack appropriate items in their trunks to take with them. Ask the first player to begin by naming something he or she will take along on the chosen trip. Each player should start by saying, "I'm going on a trip to (selected destination) and I will take. . . ."

The next player begins with the same phrase, repeats what the previous player named, and then names another appropriate item. The game continues around the circle the same way. The more players ahead of a student, the more he or she is required to remember. When a player cannot remember all the items, he or she is out.

Continue going around the circle as many times as needed until one player is left who can repeat every item said by every player, or until players cannot think of any more items to pack for their trip.

> I'm going on a trip to Germany and I will take a down vest, boots, warm clothes, an English-German dictionary, German currency, a passport, skis, goggles, maps, a camera, film, a sled, a scarf, a journal, gloves, plane tickets, . . . um . . . a tape recorder, a video camera, . . .

50

Word Origins

Name _____

Read the words listed below. Write the country or region where you think the word originated on the line next to each word. Then check your answers in a dictionary, using the Abbreviations key to identify the country names if necessary.

1. emu _____
2. kilt _____
3. gendarme _____
4. bayou _____
5. llama _____
6. kimono _____
7. drachma _____
8. Frau _____
9. queue _____
10. coup _____
11. hors d'oeuvre _____
12. gondola _____
13. mensch _____
14. calliope _____

The Great Race Game

MATERIALS:

crayons or markers scissors
letter-sized file folder glue
oaktag scraps clear contact paper
envelope die

DIRECTIONS:

1. Reproduce the game board and the ship playing pieces on pages 53–55 once. Reproduce the playing instructions once. Color the game board and four sets of playing pieces, using a different color for each set and making sure the flag atop each tent is the same color as the set of the playing pieces. The pathways to the South Pole should be colored to match each flag. Cut out.

2. Mount the ships on oaktag, laminate them, and cut out around the ships.

3. Glue the game board to the inside of a file folder. Glue the playing instructions to the front of the file folder.

4. Glue the envelope to the back of the file folder and place the game pieces and die in it for storage.

HOW TO PLAY (for 2 to 4 players)

1. Each player should choose four game pieces of the same color and place them in the Base Camp. The player rolling the lowest number on the die goes first.

2. Play moves in a clockwise direction. The first player rolls the die and moves a game piece the number of spaces shown on the die. After the first player has moved his or her piece, the player to the left goes.

3. Once a piece is out on the board, a player may choose to bring out another piece on a next turn, or bring one piece around the board at a time.

4. If a player lands on a space that is already occupied by another player's game piece, that player must take the piece off the space and put it back in his or her "Base Camp."

5. The first player to move all of his or her playing pieces around the board and up the path to the South Pole is the winner. (Each ship must land on the South Pole on an exact count.)

The Great Race Game

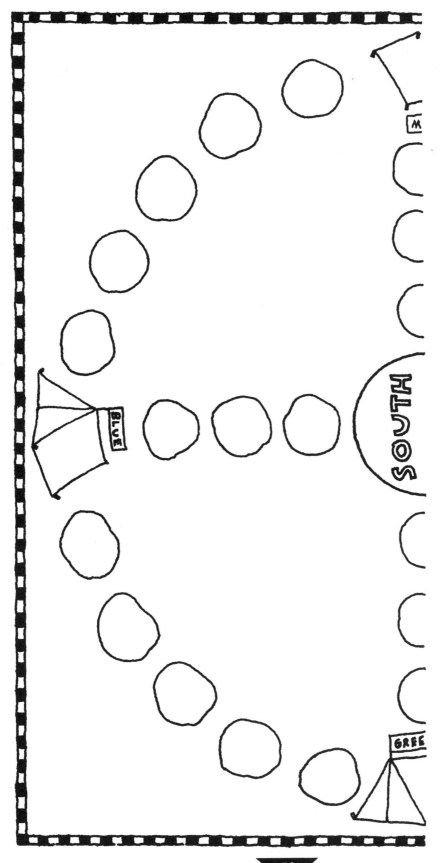

The Great Race Game

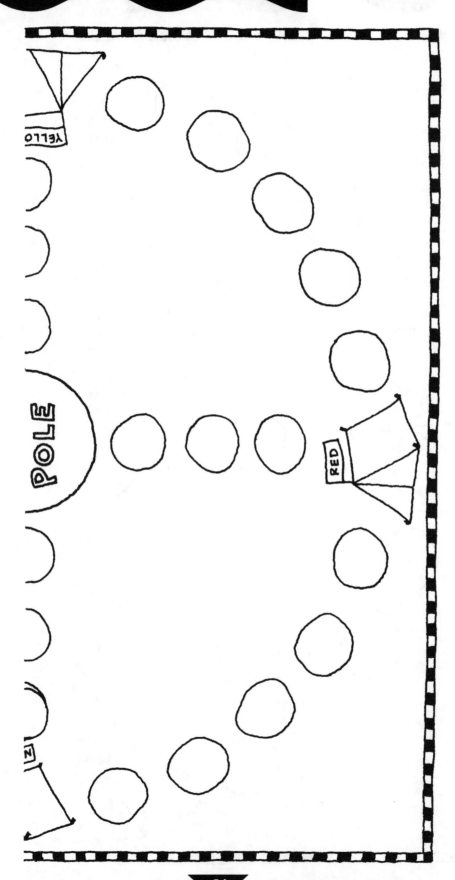

The Great Race Game

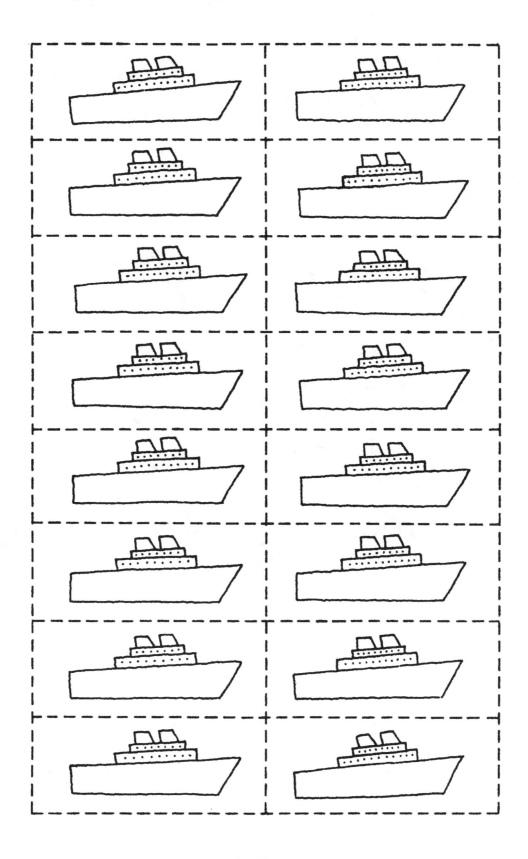

Captain Chaos

Give each student a piece of paper. Ask each child to choose two locations in the classroom or nearby (within reason). The locations should not be too close together.

Have each student write down a set of directions that would take someone from the first location to the second. The first location should be stated in the directions, but tell students to leave the destination secret. Ask students to write their names on their papers.

Collect the papers and redistribute them randomly to the class. Choose four students at a time to follow the directions on their papers.

> BEGIN AT THE CHALKBOARD NEAREST THE WINDOW. TURN TO FACE THE DOOR AND GO TO THE TEACHER'S CHAIR... STOP AT THE TRASH CAN, TURN RIGHT, AND GO FORWARD 4 FLOOR TILES. TURN LEFT AND GO TO KAREN'S DESK. TURN RIGHT AND MOVE 10 FLOOR TILES. FACE LEFT AND SIT IN THE CHAIR.

When the four students reach their destinations, have them read off the names of the students who wrote the directions. Ask those four students if the players are in the right places. If the players are correct, they may pick new players to replace them.

If a student reaches the wrong destination, ask the student to begin again, reading the directions as he or she goes. Decide where the problem lies. Depending on what the problem is, either ask the writer to fix his or her mistake or ask the player to reread the directions carefully.

Continue the game until all students have had a chance to navigate their way around the classroom.

Claim the Continent

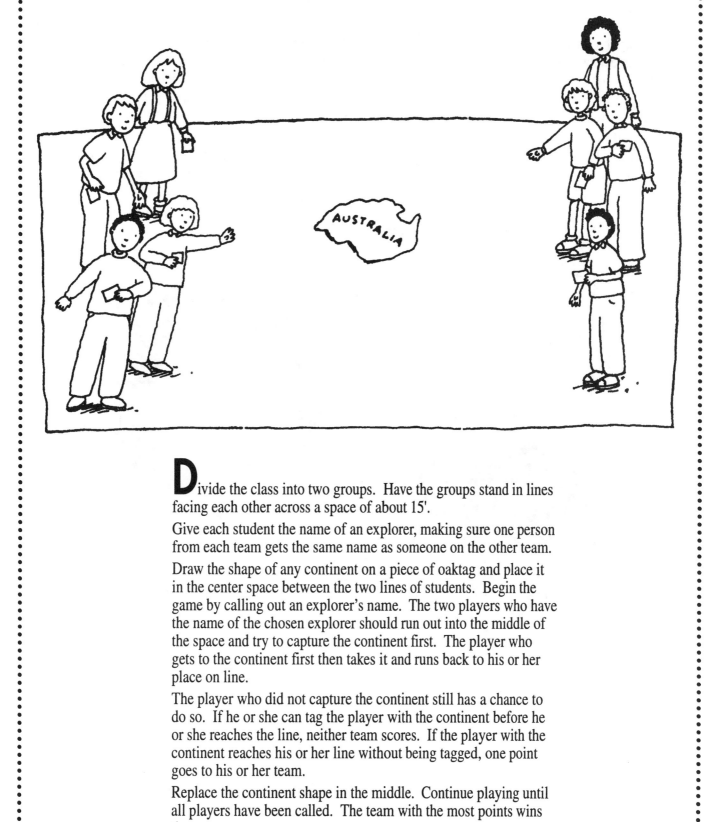

Divide the class into two groups. Have the groups stand in lines facing each other across a space of about 15'.

Give each student the name of an explorer, making sure one person from each team gets the same name as someone on the other team.

Draw the shape of any continent on a piece of oaktag and place it in the center space between the two lines of students. Begin the game by calling out an explorer's name. The two players who have the name of the chosen explorer should run out into the middle of the space and try to capture the continent first. The player who gets to the continent first then takes it and runs back to his or her place on line.

The player who did not capture the continent still has a chance to do so. If he or she can tag the player with the continent before he or she reaches the line, neither team scores. If the player with the continent reaches his or her line without being tagged, one point goes to his or her team.

Replace the continent shape in the middle. Continue playing until all players have been called. The team with the most points wins the game.

Name Connections

On half of a stack of 3" x 5" index cards, write the name of an explorer. On the other half, write an object, place, or event that is connected with each explorer's name. Make enough cards so that there is one for each student.

Shuffle all the cards together and distribute one to each student. To play, ask students to walk around the room examining their classmates' cards until they think they have found someone whose card matches their own.

When students find a match, they should sit together.

When everybody has found a match and is sitting, ask one pair at a time to stand and tell the class how their cards are connected. If students are incorrect, or if a better match can be made, they may regroup and explain again why they are connected.

This activity may played using specific categories of exploration, such as sea travel, land travel, outer space travel, deep-sea exploration, explorers who got lost, naturalists, members of a crew and their jobs, explorers who belong in a certain time period, or landmarks associated with an explorer.

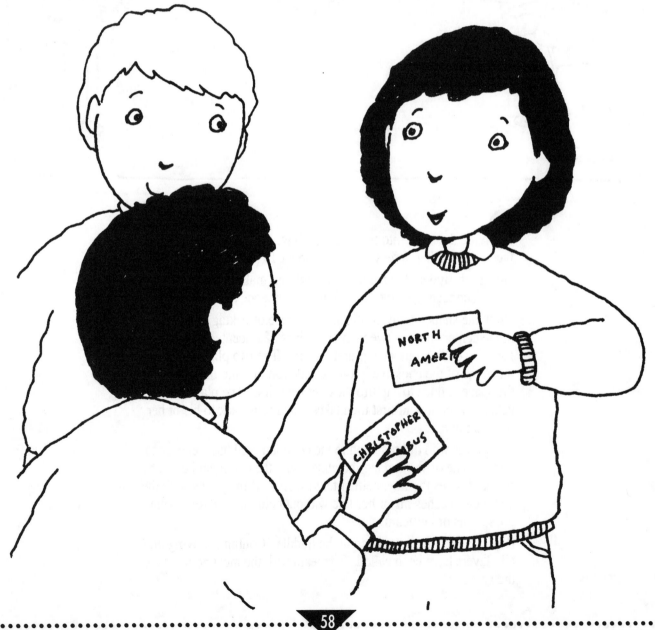

Fashion Relay Races

Collect clothing that could be associated with a particular explorer or an explorer's time period. Place three articles of clothing in each of five or six bags.

Divide the class into groups of five or six. Ask each team to stand at one end of a large, open room. Place the bags of clothing at the opposite end of the room, one across from each team.

At a signal, the first member of each team must run down to the opposite end of the room, put on the clothing in the bag, and run with the bag back to his or her team. The first player must then take off the explorer's clothing and place the clothes back in the bag, then run it back to the opposite end of the room. Finally, the player must run back to his or her team and tag the next player in line.

The race continues, with all members performing the same tasks. The first team to complete the race and sit down is the winner.

59

Mapping Skills

Name

Leif Ericson was a Viking explorer who is often credited with being the first European to set foot in North America. On the map below, draw a line showing the route he and his crew might have taken from Greenland in approximately the year 1000. Be sure to indicate any important stops along the journey.

On the back of this piece of paper, tell why you think this was an important voyage.

Mapping Skills

Name
_____

Vasco da Gama was a Portuguese explorer who sailed from Lisbon, Portugal, on July 8, 1497, to Calicut, India, arriving on May 20, 1498. On the map below show the route he took. Be sure to indicate any important stops along the journey.

On the back of this piece of paper, tell why you think this was an important voyage.

Mapping Skills

Name _____

Although Ferdinand Magellan died before his intended voyage around the world was completed, he is credited with being the inspiration and force behind this historic journey in 1519–1522. On the map below, draw a line showing the route he and his crew took. Consult an encyclopedia if you need help. Be sure to indicate any important stops along the route.

On the back of this piece of paper, tell why you think this was an important voyage.

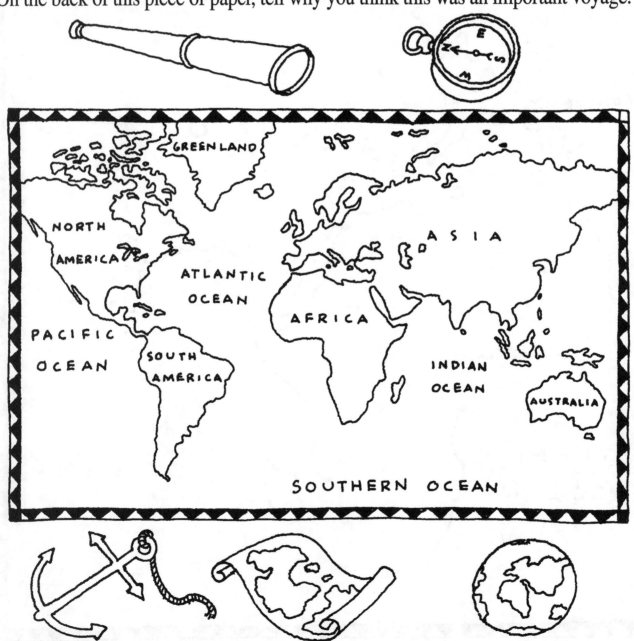

Mapping Skills

Name

Jacques Cartier was a French explorer who discovered the St. Lawrence River. On the map below, draw a line showing the route he and his crew took in 1535–1536. Consult an encyclopedia if you need help. Be sure to indicate any important stops along the route.

On the back of this piece of paper, tell why you think this was an important voyage.

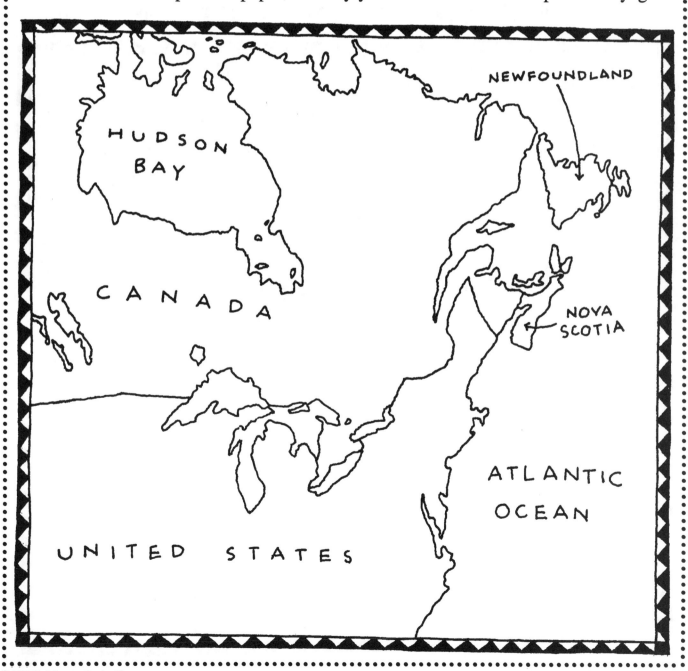

Mapping Skills

Name _____

Meriwether Lewis and William Clark led an expedition that left St. Louis, Missouri, on May 14, 1804, and traveled west to the Pacific Ocean. This journey took 18 months and opened the path for U.S. western exploration. On the map below, draw a line showing the route Lewis and Clark took. Consult an encyclopedia if you need help. Be sure to indicate any important stops along the route.

On the back of this piece of paper, tell why you think this was an important voyage.

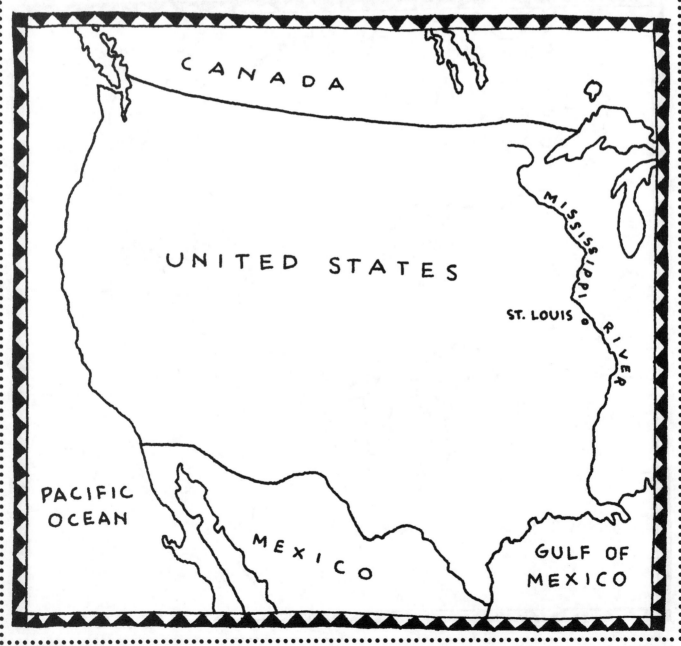

Native Tribes

Name

When European explorers arrived in the Americas, there were already Native Americans who had been living there for centuries. Consult an encyclopedia to find where the Native American tribes listed in the box below lived. Then write the name of each Native American group in the approximate location of their lands.

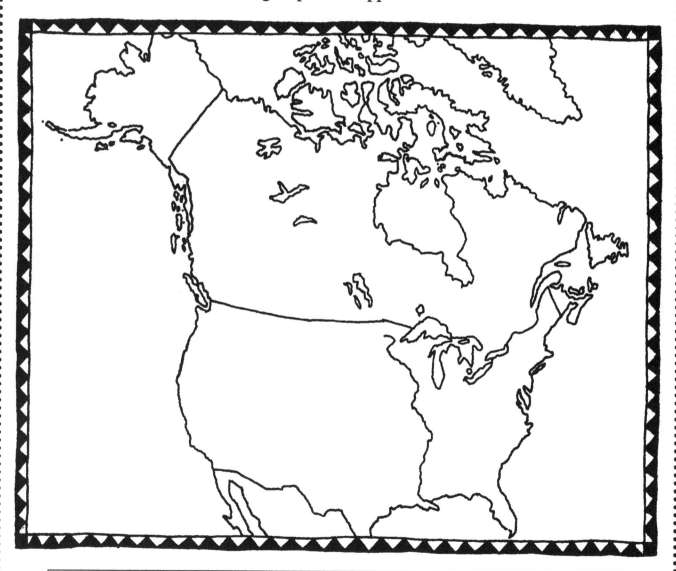

Cherokee	Huron	Osage	Apache	Shoshoni	Nez Percé
Cree	Eskimo	Chinook	Sioux	Plains Cree	Miami
Delaware	Iroquois	Seminole	Mohave	Pueblo	Blackfoot
Hopi	Chippewa	Navajo			

Best Books About Exploration

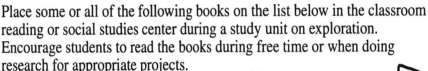
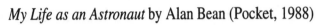

Place some or all of the following books on the list below in the classroom reading or social studies center during a study unit on exploration. Encourage students to read the books during free time or when doing research for appropriate projects.

My Life as an Astronaut by Alan Bean (Pocket, 1988)

Captain Cook by Alan Blackwood (Watts, 1987)

Daniel Boone by Keith Brandt (Troll, 1983)

Marco Polo by Gian Paolo Ceserani (Putnam, 1982)

Exploring the American West by James Collins (Watts, 1989)

Columbus by Ingri and Edgar D'Aulaire (Doubleday, 1987)

Explorers by Dennis B. Fradin (Childrens Press, 1984)

Brendan the Navigator: A History Mystery About the Discovery of America by Jean Fritz (Putnam, 1979)

Jacques Cousteau by Genie Iverson (Putnam, 1976)

Who Really Discovered America? by Stephen Krensky (Hastings, 1988)

Explorers by Keith Lye (Silver Burdett, 1984)

Early Exploration of North America by Frederick King Poole (Watts, 1989)

Explorers and Discovery by Cass R. Sandak (Watts, 1983)

Davy Crockett: Young Pioneer by Laurence Santrey (Troll, 1983)

Neil Armstrong: Space Pioneer by Paul Westman (Lerner, 1980)

Thor Heyerdahl: Across the Seas of Time by Paul Westman (Dillon, 1982)

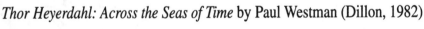
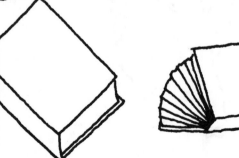

Historical Fiction

Introducing historical fiction to students is a good way to help them understand what the world was like during a certain period. For example, read the book *The True Confessions of Charlotte Doyle* by Avi (Avon, 1990) with the class. This tale, set in 1832, tells the story of a 13-year-old girl who crosses the Atlantic Ocean on a ship captained by a ruthless murderer. The girl is caught between a mutinous crew and an evil man.

Ask volunteers to talk about the setting of this novel. Some suggested questions:

> What kind of a family is Charlotte from?
> Why was she attending school in England?
> How is the setting different from a modern setting?
> Why did the sailors treat Charlotte as an outcast?
> Why were Charlotte's parents upset when she returned home?
> What kind of life do you think Charlotte led after she returned to the ship? What kind of life do you think she would have led had she remained at home?

Tell students that they will be keeping journals for their own imaginary voyages. Ask each student to choose a departure point and a destination. Encourage them to write some background information about their fictional families and the settings of their stories. Each day, have each student write what happened to him or her that day on the "ship." After several weeks, tell students that their voyages will soon be ending. Give the class a week to prepare the endings for their journals.

Ask volunteers to share their journals with the rest of the class. If desired, allow students to make covers for their journals, then place them in the reading or social studies center for all to see.

Charlotte's Glossary

Name _____

After reading *The True Confessions of Charlotte Doyle*, look at the list of words below. Write a definition for each word. Use a dictionary if you need help.

1. fathom _____
_____

2. fortnight _____
_____

3. spar (noun) _____
_____

4. exhilarating _____
_____

5. flog _____
_____

6. mutiny _____
_____

7. disembarkation _____
_____

8. port _____
_____

9. parlor _____
_____

10. outlandish _____
_____

Front-Page News

Name _____

Pretend that you are a reporter in Providence, Rhode Island, in 1832. Write a newspaper story that tells what happened to Charlotte Doyle in her adventure on board the *Seahawk*. Remember to address the five *W*'s (Who, What, Why, Where, When) and How when writing your story. If necessary, continue the story on the back of this sheet.

Providence News

May 18, 1832   Vol. 17   No. 32   3¢

_____

_____

_____

_____

_____

_____

_____

_____

_____

_____

_____

_____

_____

_____

Class Explorers Mural

MATERIALS:

large sheet of construction paper
mural paper
crayons or markers
paints and paintbrushes
tape

DIRECTIONS:

1. Divide the class into five groups. Have each group cover a different period of exploration from the 10th century through present times.

2. Ask each group to research several explorers from their time period. Have students find out what the explorer looked liked, how he or she dressed, how the explorer's party traveled, and what things he or she discovered.

3. On scrap paper, let each group sketch out a scene for their explorer. When a group is satisfied with its sketch, have the group transfer the sketch to a large piece of mural paper.

4. Provide students with crayons or markers and paints to use to color their murals. When each mural is completed, have the group write the time period featured across the top.

5. Attach the murals together in chronological order along a school hallway. Use construction paper to make a banner to put across the top of the mural time line that says "Exploration Through the Ages."

Oral Presentations

Remind students that every explorer had to find funding for his or her travels. Christopher Columbus was turned down several times before he finally persuaded Queen Isabella of Spain to give him money and ships. Part of their agreement was that he would bring back riches (jewels and spices) for Spain, and Isabella promised that she would appoint Columbus governor of newly discovered regions.

Discuss other explorers and the people who funded their travels. Allow students time to research the funding arrangements for these journeys in the school library.

When students have completed their research, divide the class into pairs. Ask each pair of students to choose an explorer and the person or group of people who funded his or her voyage. Tell students that they will be presenting skits that show what might have taken place when an explorer requested money.

Encourage the pairs to write down their dialogues. Give the pairs plenty of time to practice their parts. When everyone is prepared, schedule three or four pairs a day to present their dialogues. Allow time after each dialogue for questions from the audience.

Mr. Stanley, your next assignment for this newspaper is to find David Livingstone.

I'll need supplies, money, transportation, and a crew for my expedition.

Overseas Riches Game

MATERIALS:

crayons or markers scissors
glue letter-sized file folder
oaktag clear contact paper
envelope penny, nickel, dime, and quarter
number cube

What explorer discovered the St. Lawrence River?

Jacques Cartie[r]

DIRECTIONS:

1. Reproduce the game board on pages 73–74 once. Color the game board, cut it out, and mount it on the inside of a letter-sized file folder.

2. Reproduce the question game cards on page 75 three times. Write a question on each card that deals with the unit of exploration the class is currently studying. Write the answer on the back of each card. Mount the game cards on oaktag, laminate them, and cut them out.

3. Reproduce the "riches" game cards on page 76 twice. Color the cards, laminate them, and cut them out.

4. Reproduce the "How to Play" instructions on this page once. Cut out the instructions and glue them to the front of the file folder.

5. Use a penny, nickel, dime, and quarter as playing pieces. Glue an envelope to the back of the file folder. Use the envelope to store the game cards, playing pieces, and a number cube.

HOW TO PLAY:

(for two to four players)

1. Shuffle the question game cards and place them in a pile with the questions faceup in the center of the game board. Shuffle the "riches" game cards and place them in a stack next to the game board. Players place their playing pieces on Start.

2. Play moves clockwise around the board. The youngest player goes first and rolls the number cube. That player moves the indicated number of spaces on the game board. If the player lands on a star, he or she may draw a game card and read the question aloud. If the player answers the question correctly, he or she may choose one of the riches from the pile next to the game board. If the player answers incorrectly, his or her turn is over.

3. The player to the first player's left goes next. Play continues until one player reaches Finish. The player with the most "riches" cards is the winner.

Overseas Riches Game

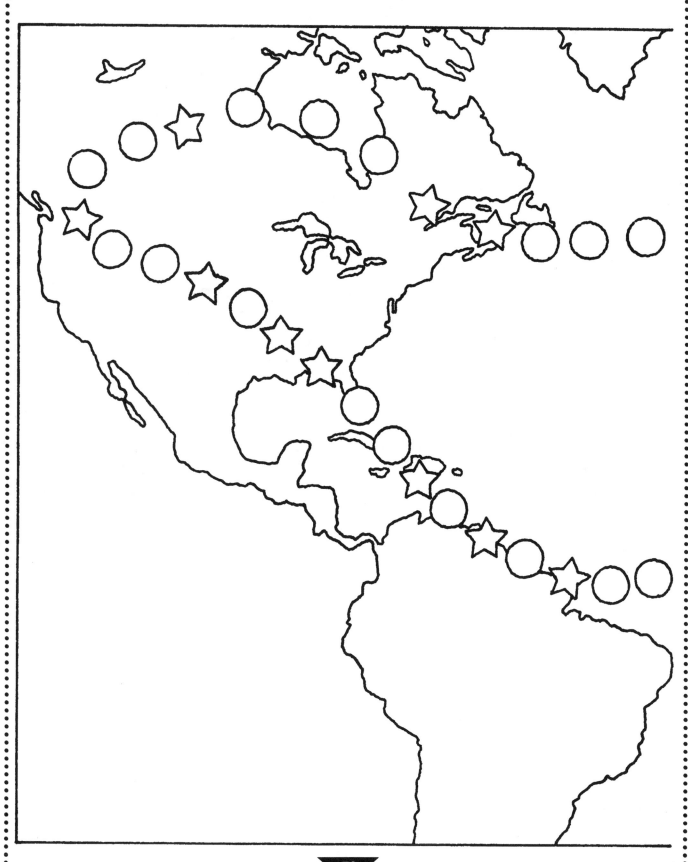

Overseas Riches Game

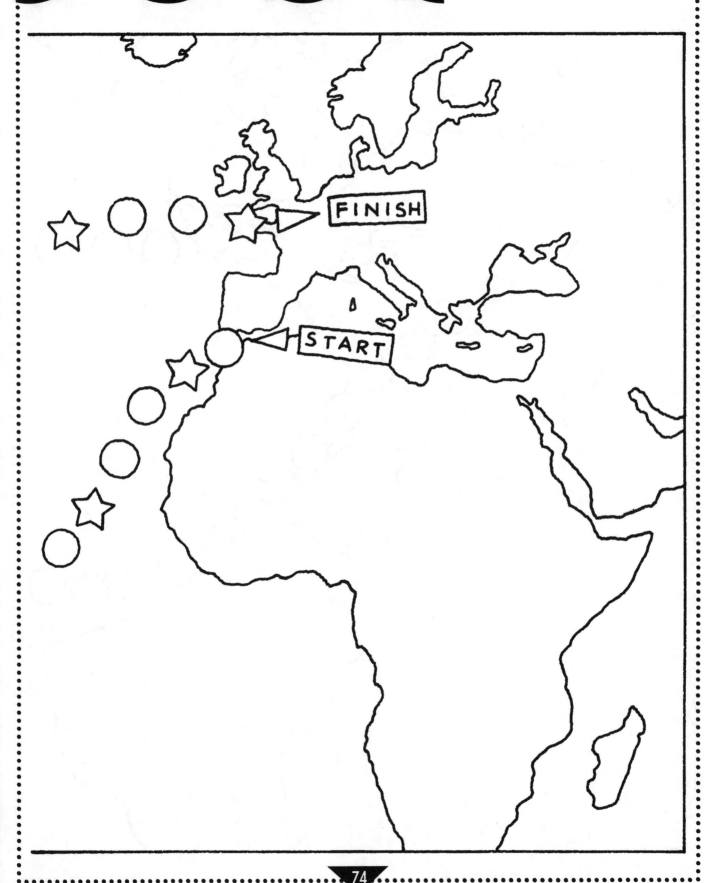

Overseas Riches Game

Overseas Riches Game

What If . . . ?

Give students a different "What if . . .?" writing topic each week when studying a particular explorer. For example, if the class is working on a study unit about Cortés, you may ask "What if the Aztecs had defeated the Spaniards? How would this have changed history?"

Allow approximately 20 minutes for students to write rough drafts of their essays. Or give the assignment as homework and let them write as long as they like.

Review the rough draft individually with each student. Point out places where his or her story needs work, as well as spelling and grammatical errors.

After students write their final drafts, ask them to draw pictures to go along with their stories. Place the stories in the social studies center for all to enjoy.

If desired, ask students to suggest new "What if . . .?" topics. Place students' suggestions in a box and draw a new one randomly each week.

77

Name Boxes

Name _____

Each of the boxes below has one explorer's name hidden in it. To discover which explorer is in each one, start at the arrow in each box. Draw a line from letter to letter until you have completed the explorer's name. The first one has been done for you.

1.

→
C	M	A	C
S	O	L	U
R	A	T	M
I	N	B	T
S	U	A	B

Columbus

2.

→
M	A	L	B
M	G	O	R
E	C	E	S
T	W	A	L
S	N	A	L

_____

3.

→
B	M	T	R
A	W	G	E
B	L	O	L
S	B	S	L
T	O	A	N

_____

4.

→
D	A	O	A
S	Z	G	V
O	P	A	C
R	M	R	U
A	C	O	L

_____

5.

→
H	C	L	E
U	D	E	N
M	S	D	R
O	A	G	W
N	T	S	Y

_____

6.

→
P	E	C	L
A	T	R	K
T	R	C	S
S	W	Y	W
L	E	S	R

_____

Yum, Yum!

Name _____

As a result of the discoveries of European explorers, many new and exotic foods and spices were brought to Europe. Unscramble the words below to see which new foods were enjoyed by happy European diners!

1. EPPEINPAL _____

2. TOPTAO _____

3. OTLINCAR _____

4. EEPPRP _____

5. COOAEHCLT _____

6. RONC _____

7. EETWS OAOSPTTE _____

8. RASGU _____

9. NAABNA _____

10. STUNAEP _____

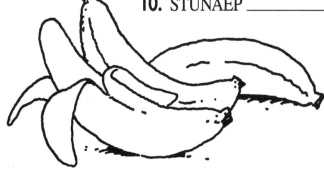

Animals of the World

Name _____

The European explorers discovered many new and different kinds of animals in North and South America. Look at the list of animals below. Next to each name, write the region to which the animal is indigenous, or native.

1. horse _____

2. coyote _____

3. bighorn sheep _____

4. cattle _____

5. bison _____

6. chinchilla _____

7. giant panda _____

8. kangaroo _____

9. ostrich _____

10. moose _____

11. red deer _____

12. koala _____

13. raccoon _____

14. otter _____

15. bobcat _____

Countries of Origin

Name _____

Read the list of explorers below. On the lines provided, write the name of the country from which each explorer came. (Use the box at the bottom of the page to help you.)

1. Vasco Núñez de Balboa _____
2. Henry Hudson _____
3. Vasco da Gama _____
4. Christopher Columbus _____
5. Leif Ericson _____
6. Ferdinand Magellan _____
7. Meriwether Lewis _____
8. Hernando Cortes _____
9. Bartholomeu Dias _____
10. Francisco Pizarro _____

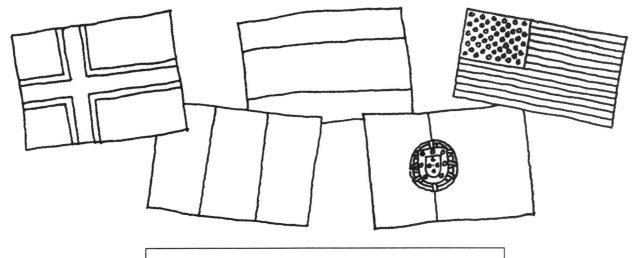

Italy	United States	Norway
Spain	England	Portugal

Mystery Guests

Assign a different explorer to each student in the class. Tell students to keep the names of their explorers secret.

Ask the children to research their explorers. Allow time for students to go to the school library to find out information about their explorers, such as:

- birth date and birthplace
- country of origin
- education
- country for which he or she explored
- voyages
- important discoveries
- date and reason for death

When everyone has sufficiently prepared, ask students to come up one at a time in front of the class to portray their explorers. Tell the class that they may ask "Yes" or "No" questions of each student to find out the name of his or her explorer.

Allow a certain number of questions (for example, 15) before asking the class to guess the name of the explorer. Students may guess earlier in the game, if desired. If a student guesses the name of an explorer and is incorrect, he or she may not ask any further questions. If a student guesses correctly, he or she becomes the next player.

Continue playing until everyone has had a turn. If desired, play the game with other classes studying similar units of exploration.

Imaginations on the Run

Give the class a list of exploration topics to use for a creative writing assignment. Some suggestions are:

> You are a young Incan boy or girl. You see the Spaniards approaching on horseback.
> You are a cabin boy for Magellan as he sets sail to circumnavigate the globe.
> You are a merchant who is selling supplies to Lewis and Clark as they prepare for their westward journey.
> You are a news reporter interviewing Columbus after his return to Spain.
> You are Leif Ericson's son or daughter and are awaiting his return from Vinland.
> You are first mate on Hudson's ship as it becomes locked in ice in Hudson Bay.
> You are a Native American on a Caribbean island who spots three large ships in the distance.

Encourage the children to do research to find as many historical facts as possible to include in their stories. Tell students to use dialogue and descriptive language.

Have the children write rough drafts of their stories. Then go over the draft with each student, pointing out any problems with content, spelling, and grammar.

Tell students to copy their final drafts onto white lined paper. Ask each student to make a picture to go with his or her story. Attach the stories and pictures to a bulletin board under the heading "Imaginative Adventures."

Who Did That?

FOUNTAIN OF YOUTH

Name _____

Read the names of the explorers in the column on the left. Then draw a line to match each explorer to the item on the right for which he is known.

1. Jacques Cartier

2. Vasco da Gama

3. Amerigo Vespucci

4. Ponce de León

5. Francisco de Coronado

6. Hernando de Soto

7. Sir Francis Drake

8. James Cook

9. Samuel de Champlain

10. Louis Jolliet

a. First English explorer to sail around the world

b. Sailed to the West Indies and South America; America was named after him

c. Searched for the "fountain of youth"

d. Explored the St. Lawrence River; reached Lake Champlain

e. Explored the Mississippi River

f. Sailed up the St. Lawrence River

g. First European to reach India by sea

h. Explored the Great Lakes and the Mississippi River valley

i. Explored Mexico, Texas, and the southwestern U.S.

j. Explored the South Pacific

Aztec Crossword Puzzle

Name _____

The Aztecs were a Native American people who ruled in what is now Mexico during the 1400-1500s. Read each of the clues below and fill in the appropriate words to complete the puzzle. Consult an encyclopedia if you need help.

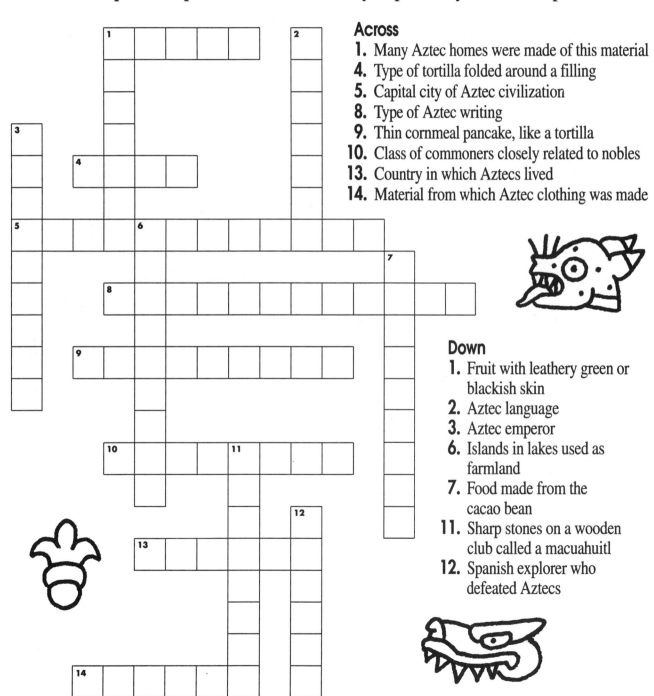

Across
1. Many Aztec homes were made of this material
4. Type of tortilla folded around a filling
5. Capital city of Aztec civilization
8. Type of Aztec writing
9. Thin cornmeal pancake, like a tortilla
10. Class of commoners closely related to nobles
13. Country in which Aztecs lived
14. Material from which Aztec clothing was made

Down
1. Fruit with leathery green or blackish skin
2. Aztec language
3. Aztec emperor
6. Islands in lakes used as farmland
7. Food made from the cacao bean
11. Sharp stones on a wooden club called a macuahuitl
12. Spanish explorer who defeated Aztecs

DIRECTIONS:

- crayons or markers
- glue
- oaktag
- scissors
- pushpins or thumbtacks
- construction paper (optional)

MATERIALS:

1. Reproduce the figures on pages 87–89 once. Color the figures, mount them on oaktag, and cut them out.

2. Attach the figures to a bulletin board under the heading "Famous American Adventurers." You may wish to attach them to a time line, as shown, or ran-domly. Leave room around each explorer for student essays.

3. Ask each student to choose one of the famous Americans. Have each child read a biography about the selected person and then write an essay about the part of the adventurer's life that he or she finds most interesting.

4. Attach the essays near the appropriate adventurer.

5. As an alternate activity, reproduce the selected adventurer once for each child. Have students glue the figure to a piece of construction paper and use it as a cover for a book he or she has written about the adventurer.

American Adventurers

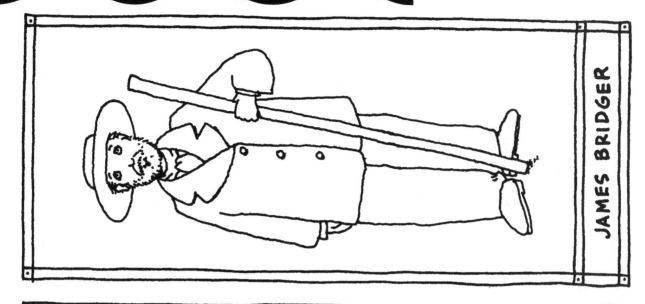

JAMES BRIDGER

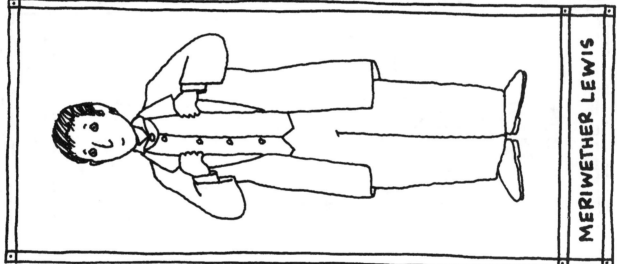

MERIWETHER LEWIS

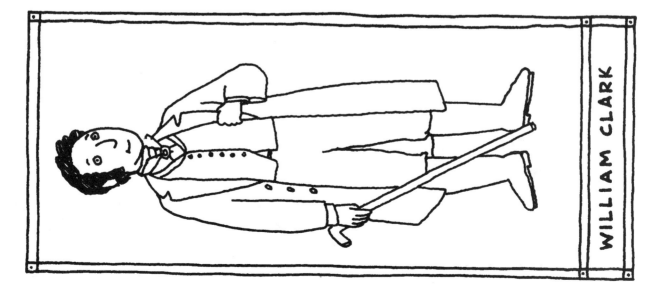

WILLIAM CLARK

American Adventurers

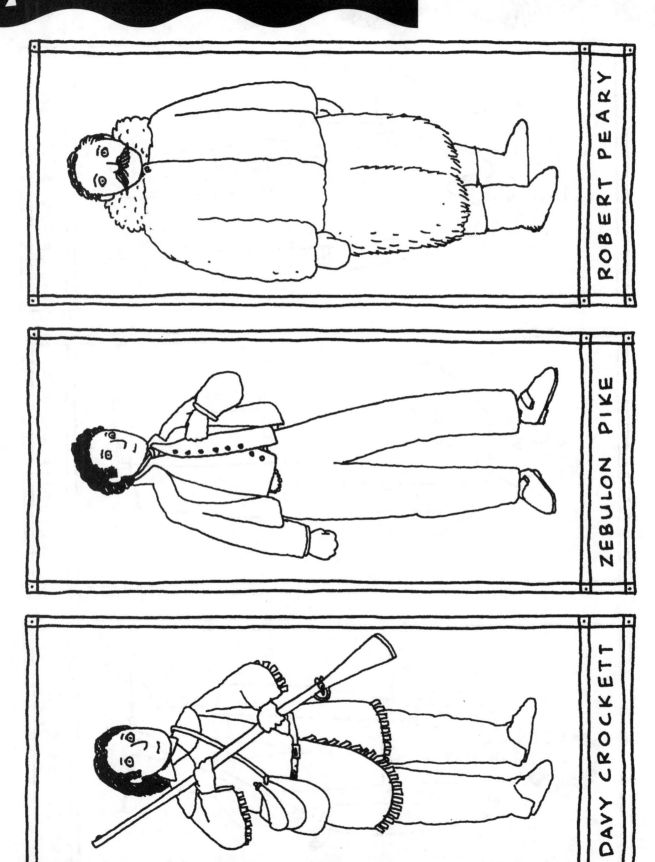

ROBERT PEARY

ZEBULON PIKE

DAVY CROCKETT

American Adventurers

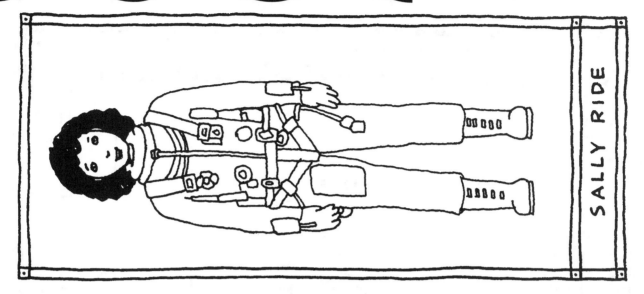

SALLY RIDE

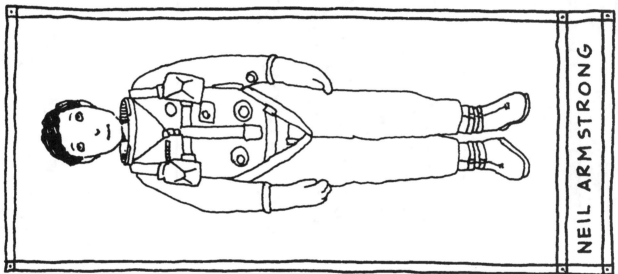

NEIL ARMSTRONG

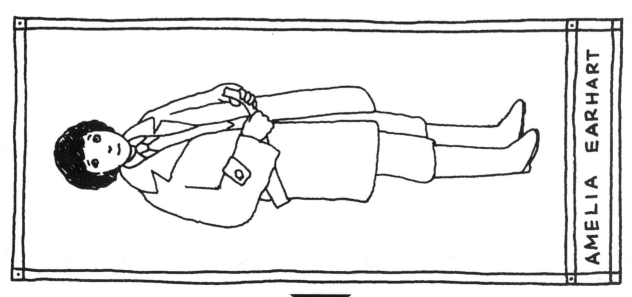

AMELIA EARHART

PRESENTED TO

_____

FOR BRAVERY AND COURAGE

IN DISCOVERING INFORMATION ABOUT

_____

PRESENTED BY _____ DATE _____

PRESENTED TO

FOR

RESEARCH SKILLS

IN DISCOVERING INFORMATION ABOUT

SIGNED

DATE

Answers

page 12

1. Henry the Navigator
2. thirteenth
3. 1804—1806
4. walk on the moon
5. Amelia Earhart
6. 1911
7. 1893
8. 1984
9. Vinland
10. Queen Hatshepsut

page 13

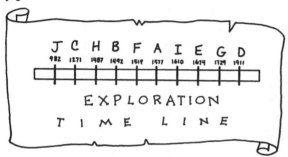

J C H B F A I E G D
982 1271 1487 1492 1519 1557 1610 1674 1729 1911

EXPLORATION
TIME LINE

page 17

Air	Sea	Land
butterfly	porcupine fish	kangaroo
bee	dolphin	elephant
	penguin	giraffe
		penguin
		panda
		rattlesnake

page 19

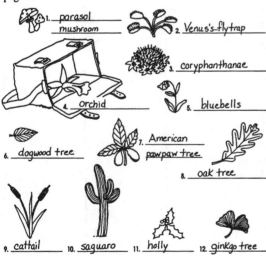

1. parasol mushroom
2. Venus's-fly-trap
3. coryphanthanae
4. orchid
5. bluebells
6. dogwood tree
7. American pawpaw tree
8. oak tree
9. cattail
10. saguaro
11. holly
12. ginkgo tree

page 22

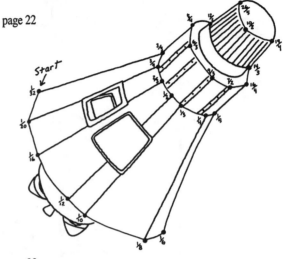

Start

page 23

Answers will vary.

page 24

1. 250 ounces; 15.625 pounds
2. no; 15 yards
3. 1 bag of cinnamon; yes—1 piece
4. 2 silver bowls
5. 13 pieces
6. convert pieces of gold to ounces of gold (330 ounces of gold); 33; no

page 25

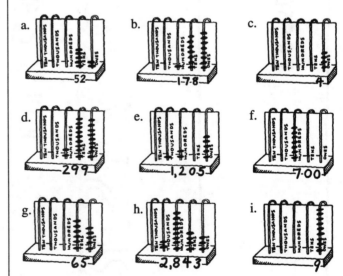

a. 52
b. 1·78
c. 4·
d. 299
e. 1,205·
f. 7·00·
g. 65·
h. 2,843·
i. 9·

Answers

page 26

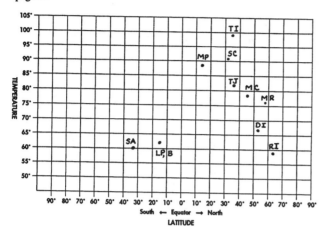

page 27

1. Manila and LaPaz
2. Sydney and Reykjavik; 2 degrees Fahrenheit and about 99 degrees latitude
3. Shanghai and Tokyo
4. Moscow and Dublin
5. because it is the farthest north of the listed cities
6. 2; Sydney and La Paz
7. 50
8. 80 (Tehran, Manila, and Shanghai)

page 28

1. Orion—Northern Hemisphere
2. Big Dipper—Northern Hemisphere
3. Little Dipper—Northern Hemisphere
4. Cassiopeia—Northern Hemisphere
5. Andromeda—Northern Hemisphere

page 29

1. Pluto, Mercury, Mars, Venus, Earth, Neptune, Uranus, Saturn, Jupiter.
2. Mercury, Venus, Earth, Mars, Jupiter, Saturn, Uranus, Neptune, Pluto.
3. 4,380
4. Jupiter
5. 31 million miles; 402 million miles; 3 billion, 607 million miles

page 31

1. 9,000
2. Warsaw
3. Melbourne to Cape Town
4. about 3 days
5. Chicago—Mexico City—Caracas—Lima; about 7,000 miles
6. Melbourne to Caracas
7. 7,500
8. 6,000 miles
9. Lima to New Delhi
10. 15,000 miles

page 32

1. 657
2. 4,445
3. 1,000
4. 11,001,589,298
5. 1,889
6. 13,560
7. 375
8. 4,489

Message: You will find stalagmites, bats, lakes, and lime.

page 33

1. 150
2. 1,500; 300
3. 125
4. 2 bear skins
5. 450
6. 126 days; about 4 months
7. yes
8. Answers will vary. Possible answers include 96 beaver pelts/60 bear skins.

page 40

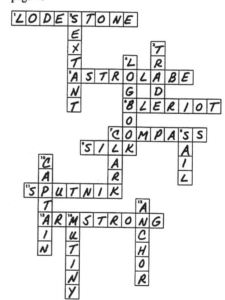

page 44

Answers will vary.

page 51

1. Portugal
2. Scandinavia
3. France
4. United States
5. Spain (Andes)
6. Japan
7. Greece
8. Germany
9. France
10. France
11. France
12. Italy
13. Germany
14. Greece

Answers

page 60

page 61

page 62

page 63

page 64

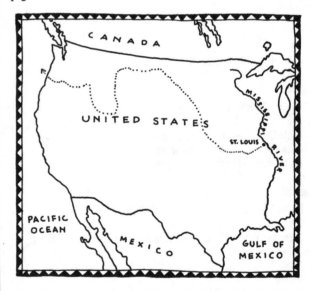

Answers

page 65

page 68

1. fathom—a unit of measurement that equals 6 feet.
2. fortnight—two weeks.
3. spar—a pole that supports the rigging of a ship.
4. exhilarating—stimulating or invigorating.
5. flog—to beat with a whip or a rod.
6. mutiny—rebellion of a ship's crew against their captain or officers.
7. disembarkation—leaving a ship and going onto the shore.
8. port—a harbor where a ship docks.
9. parlor—a room in a house where guests are received.
10. outlandish—unconventional or absurd.

page 78

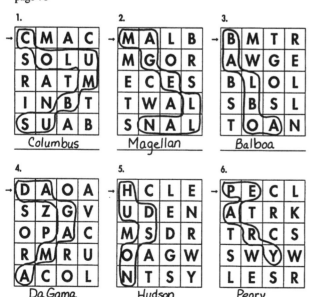

page 79

1. pineapple
2. potato
3. cilantro
4. pepper
5. chocolate
6. corn
7. sweet potatoes
8. sugar
9. banana
10. peanuts

page 80

1. Europe, Asia
2. United States, Canada, Mexico
3. North America
4. Asia, Europe
5. North America
6. Peru, Bolivia, Chile
7. China
8. Australia
9. Africa
10. North America, Europe, Asia
11. Europe, Asia, North Africa
12. Australia
13. North America, South America
14. North America, South America, Europe, Africa, Asia
15. North America

page 81

1. Spain
2. England
3. Portugal
4. Italy, but he explored for Spain
5. Norway
6. Portugal and Spain
7. United States
8. Spain
9. Portugal
10. Spain

page 84

1. f
2. g
3. b
4. c
5. i
6. e
7. a
8. j
9. d
10. h

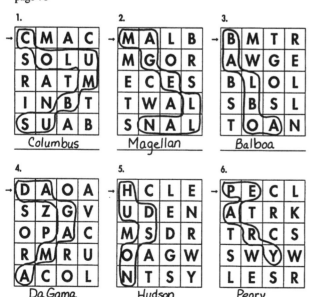

Answers

page 85

```
            ¹A  D  O  B  E      ²N
            V                    A
            O                    H
 ³M         C          ⁴T  A  C  O  U
 O      ⁴T  A  C  O              A
 N          D                    T
 ⁵T  E  N  O  ⁶C  H  T  I  T  L  A  N
 E          H                       ⁷C
 Z      ⁸P  I  C  T  O  G  R  A  P  H  I  C
 U          N                       O
 M      ⁹T  L  A  X  C  A  L  L  I  C
 A          M                       O
            P                       L
        ¹⁰C  A  L  P  ¹¹O  L  L  I   A
            S          B            T
                       S   ¹²C       E
        ¹³M  E  X  I  C   O  R
            D          R
            I          T
            A          E
        ¹⁴C  O  T  T  O  N   S
```